D1294492

ARAN & FAIR ISLE KNITTING

CHARTWELL
BOOKS INC.

SPINNERS' ADDRESSES

American Thread and **Dawn** yarns by – American Thread, High Ridge Park, Stamford, Connecticut 06905.

Bear Brand, Botany, Bucilla and **Fleisher** yarns by – Bernhard Ulmann Co., Division of Indian Head, 30-20 Thomson Avenue, Long Island City, New York 11101.

Bernat yarns by – Emile Bernat & Sons Co., Uxbridge, Massachusetts 01569.

Brunswick yarns by – Brunswick Yarns, 230 Fifth Avenue, New York, New York 10001.

Coats & Clark's yarns by – Coats & Clark's, 430 Park Avenue, New York, New York 10022.

Columbia Minerva yarns by – Columbia-Minerva Corp., 295 Fifth Avenue, New York, New York 10016.

Lily yarns by – Lily Mills Co., Shelby, N.C. 28150.

Melrose Yarn Co. Inc. 1305 Utica Avenue, Brooklyn, New York 11203.

Reynolds yarns by – Reynolds Yarns Inc., 15 Oser Avenue, Hauppauge, New York 11787.

Spinnerin yarns by – Spinnerin Yarn Co. Inc., 230 Fifth Avenue, New York, New York 10001.

Unger yarns by – William Unger & Co. 230 Fifth Avenue, New York, New York 10001.

Pictures supplied by

Tony Boases	42
Stuart Brown	29
Camera Press	50
Roger Charity	13, 19, 60, 61
Monty Coles	15, 17, 21
Jean Paul Froggett	8, 9
Jeany	62
Sandra Lousada	1, 25-27, 30, 33, 36, 45, 46, 53, 58, 59
John Ryan	2-7

First published in the U K by
Marshall Cavendish Promotions Limited
58, Old Compton St London W1V 5PA

© Marshall Cavendish Limited 1974, 1975, 1976, 1977

First published in the USA, 1977

Distributed in the United States by
Chartwell Books Inc.
a division of Book Sales Inc.,
110 Enterprise Avenue, Secaucus, NJ 07074, U S A

0–89009–110–2

Some of the material first appeared in the publications Fashion Maker and Aran & Fair Isle Knitting.

Printed in the United States of America.

This Edition is not to be sold outside the United States of America and the Philippines.

ABBREVIATIONS

alt	alternate(ly)	**patt**	pattern
approx	approximate(ly)	**psso**	pass slipped stitch over
beg	begin(ning)	**P-wise**	purlwise
ch	chain(s)	**rem**	remain(ing)
cl	cluster	**rep**	repeat
cm	centimeter(s)	**RS**	right side
cont	continu(e) (ing)	**sc**	single crochet
dec	decrease	**sl**	slip
dc	double crochet	**sl st**	slip stitch in knitting
dtr	double treble	**ss**	slip stitch in crochet
foll	follow(ing)	**sp(s)**	space(s)
g st	garter stitch, every row knit	**st(s)**	stitch(es)
grm	gram(s)	**st st**	Stockinette stitch, 1 row knit, 1 row purl
gr(s)	group(s)	**tbl**	through back of loop
hdc	half double	**tog**	together
in	inch(es)	**tr**	treble
inc	increase	**WS**	wrong side
K	knit	**yd(s)**	yard(s)
K-wise	knitwise	**ybk**	yarn back
No.	number	**yfwd**	yarn forward
P	purl	**yon**	yarn over needle
		yrn	yarn round needle

Symbols

An asterisk, *, shown in a pattern row denotes that the stitches shown after this sign must be repeated from that point.
Square brackets, [ ], denote instructions for larger sizes in the pattern.
Round brackets, ( ), denote that this section of the pattern is to be worked for all sizes.

GAUGE

Gauge is the most important factor in successful knitting and crochet. Unless you obtain the correct gauge given for these designs you will not obtain satisfactory results.

KNITTING NEEDLE SIZES

USA	Metric	English
—	2mm	14
0	2¼mm	13
1	2¾mm	12
2	3mm	11
3	3¼mm	10
4	3¾mm	9
5	4mm	8
6	4½mm	7
7	5mm	6
8	5½mm	5
9	6mm	4
10	6½mm	3
10½	7mm	2
11	7½mm	1
—	8mm	0
13	9mm	00
15	10mm	000

About this book

raditional knitting designs are very much in vogue the moment. 'Ethnic' knitting is high fashion and e traditional designs from the Aran and Fair Isles e every bit as ethnic as those from South America, Mexico and Afghanistan high on the fashion charts st now.

Extraordinary though it may seem, each of the esign motifs in Aran knitting—every combination f twist, bobble and cable—has a meaning of its own, me of them dating back to several centuries ago. riginally the combination of these patterns in any ven sweater served as a means of identifying dividual fishermen who might be lost at sea. As me went on, more symbolic embellishments were ded, representing such things as the ups and owns of married life (and there were many!),

geographical features such as rocky cliffs or sheltered havens, religious symbols even the twist of a fisherman's rope. Each Aran sweater was a story in itself, a rich tapestry of life created by the women who stayed at home.

Fair Isle patterns, worked in the soft muted shades of that region's vegetation, formed the traditional decorative yokes of the warm and beautiful knitwear worn by the islanders. Nowadays, these have been adapted for more brightly colored yarns and many new designs now qualify as Fair Isle. Traditional or modern, both are highly fashionable and suit all ages.

Neither Aran nor Fair Isle knitting is easy, but both would make superb—and timeless—additions to your knitting wardrobe.

Contents

Aran and Fair Isle

Aran and Fair Isle are both traditional designs which trace their origins through centuries of fine craftsmanship. Traditional Aran includes symbolic combinations of stitches which weave stories of everyday life. Fair Isle designs have been used to add decorative borders in long established color combinations. Neither of these designs is easy, but if you are not an experienced knitter – do not be daunted! – we include a comprehensive stitch guide which covers both the traditional Aran combinations and the crossed, cable and bobble stitches which you will need to understand before you begin.

Similarly all the Fair Isle border patterns plus modern interpretations are included in our Fair Isle library.

But that's not all – Aran and Fair Isle Knitting has a carefully chosen Aran and Fair Isle design collection for men, women – even the baby.

You will be enchanted by these designs and you will be helping to keep a traditional art form alive.

Aran stitch library

Crossed stitches

Crossed stitches which have a twisted appearance are used extensively in Aran patterns and the same methods may be used to create effective miniature and mock cable patterns. Because only two, or at most three, stitches are crossed at any one time, it is not necessary to use a cable needle, so these patterns are simple to work.

Crossed stitches should be knitted against a purl background to show to their best advantage, but to produce an even tighter twist on the stitches, it is also necessary to know how to twist them on the wrong side, or on a purl row against a knitted background.

Knitted crossed stitches with back twist
The crossed stitches are worked over two knitted stitches and the twist lies to the left. Pass the right hand needle behind the first stitch on the left hand needle, knit into the back of the next stitch on the left hand needle then knit into the front of the first missed stitch and slip both stitches off the left hand needle together. The abbreviation for this is 'T2B'

Mock cable
Cast on a number of stitches divisible by 5 + 3.

1st row P3, *K2, P3, rep from * to end.
2nd row K3, *P2, K3, rep from * to end.
Rep 1st and 2nd rows once more.
5th row P3, *T2B, P3, rep from * to end.
6th row As 2nd.
These 6 rows form the pattern.

Twisted rib
Cast on a number of stitches divisible by 14 + 2.
1st row P2, *T2B, P2, K4, P2, T2B, P2, rep from * to end.
2nd row K2, *P2, K2, P4, K2, P2, K2, rep from * to end.
Rep 1st and 2nd rows once more.
5th row P2, *T2B, P2, into 4th and 3rd sts on left hand needle work T2B leaving sts on needle then work T2B into 2nd and 1st sts and sl all 4 sts off needle tog, P2, T2B, P2, rep from * to end.
6th row As 2nd.
These 6 rows form the pattern.

Knitted crossed stitches with front twist

The crossed stitches are worked over two knitted stitches and the twist lies to the right. Pass the right hand needle in front of the first stitch on the left hand needle, knit into the front of the next stitch on the left hand needle then knit into the front of the first missed stitch and slip both stitches off the needle together. The abbreviation for this is 'T2F'.

Three stitches can be crossed in the same way by working into the 3rd stitch, then into 2nd and then into the first, slipping all 3 stitches off the left hand needle together. The abbreviation for this is 'T3F'.

Twisted panels

Cast on a number of stitches divisible by 8 + 2.
1st row P2, *(T2F) 3 times, P2, rep from * to end.
2nd row K2, *P6, K2, rep from * to end.
3rd row P2, *(T3F) twice, P2, rep from * to end.
4th row As 2nd.
These 4 rows form the pattern.

Purled crossed stitches with front twist

The crossed stitches are worked over two purled stitches and form a crossed thread lying to the right on the knitted side of the work. Pass the right hand needle in front of the first stitch on the left hand needle and purl the next stitch on the left hand needle, purl the first missed stitch and slip both stitches off the left hand needle together. The abbreviation for this is 'T2PF'.

Purled crossed stitches with back twist

The crossed stitches are worked over two purled stitches and form a crossed thread lying to the left on the knitted side of the work. Pass the right hand needle behind the first stitch on the left hand needle and purl the next stitch on the left hand needle through the back of the loop, purl the first missed stitch and slip both stitches off the left hand needle together. The abbreviation for this is 'T2PB'.

Crossing two knitted stitches to the right

Pass the right hand needle in front of the first stitch on the left hand needle and knit into the next stitch on the left hand needle, lift this stitch over the first missed stitch and off the needle then knit the first missed stitch. The abbreviation for this is 'C2R'.

Crossing two knitted stitches to the left

Slip the first stitch on to the right hand needle without knitting it, knit the next stitch on the left hand needle and slip it on to the right hand needle, using the left hand needle point pass the first slipped stitch over the knitted stitch, knitting into the slipped stitch at the same time. The abbreviation for this is 'C2L'.

Crossed cable

Cast on a number of stitches divisible by 7 + 3.
1st row P3, *K4, P3, rep from * to end.
2nd row K3, *P4, K3, rep from * to end.
3rd row P3, *C2R, C2L, P3, rep from * to end.
4th row As 2nd.
These 4 rows form the pattern.

Cable patterns

Cable patterns, using variations of stitches are among the most popular in knitting, since they are easy to work and give an interesting fabric with many uses — they can be thick and chunky for a sports sweater, or fine and lacy for baby garments. Twisting the cables in opposite directions can produce an all-over fabric, or simple panels of cables against the purl side of stocking stitch can give a special look to the most basic garment. All cable patterns are based on the method of moving a sequence of stitches from one position to another in a row, giving the effect of the twists you see in a rope — the more stitches moved, the thicker the rope.

We have already dealt with the method of crossing two or three stitches to give a twisted effect but when altering the position of more than two stitches, it is easier to do so by means of a third needle, which is used to hold the stitches being moved until they are ready to be worked. For this purpose a special cable needle is the best, although any short, double pointed needle will do. Cable needles are very short and manoeuvrable and are made in the same sizes as knitting needles. If the cable needle is not the same thickness as the needles being used for the garment, then it should be finer and not thicker. A thicker needle is more difficult to use and, apart from this, it will stretch the stitches and spoil the appearance of the finished work.

Cable abbreviations

Although working instructions and abbreviations will usually be found in detail in any cable pattern, before beginning to knit it would be as well to study these, as they do vary considerably. As a general guide, the letter 'C' stands for the word 'cable', followed by the number of stitches to be cabled, then the letter 'B' for back, or 'F' for front, indicating the direction in which the stitches are to be moved. In this way a cable twist from right to left over 6 stitches is abbreviated as 'C6F' and a cable twist from left to right over 6 stitches is abbreviated as 'C6B'.

Cable twist from right to left

A simple cable worked over 6 knitted stitches against a purl background. To work this sample

cast on 24 stitches.
1st row (RS) P9, K6, P9.
2nd row K9, P6, K9.
Rep 1st and 2nd rows twice more.
7th row P9, sl next 3 sts on to cable needle and hold at front of work, K next 3 sts from left hand needle then K3 sts from cable needle — called C6F —, P9.

8th row As 2nd.
These 8 rows form the pattern. Repeat pattern rows twice more. Cast off.
This sample produces a rope-like pattern in the centre, consisting of 6 knitted stitches twisted 3 times. Each twist lies in the same direction from the right to the left.

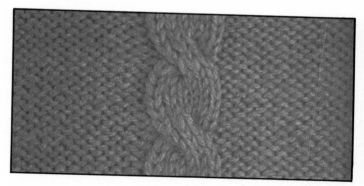

Cable twist from left to right

Cast on and work the first 6 rows as given for cable twist from right to left.
7th row P9, sl next 3 sts on to cable needle and hold at back of work, K next 3 sts from left hand needle then K3 sts from cable needle — called C6B —, P9.

8th row As 2nd.

These 8 rows form the pattern. Repeat pattern rows twice more. Cast off.

This sample will be similar to the first, but each twist will lie in the opposite direction from the left to the right.

Cable twist from right to left with row variations

The appearance of each cable twist is altered considerably by the number of rows worked between each twist. Cast on and work the first 4 rows as given for cable twist from right to left.

5th row P9, C6F, P9.

6th row As 2nd.

Rep 1st and 2nd rows twice more, then 5th and 6th rows once more.

Rep 1st and 2nd rows 4 times more, then 5th and 6th rows once more.

Rep 1st and 2nd rows 6 times more, then 5th and 6th rows once more.

Rep 1st and 2nd rows once more. Cast off.

Alternating cables

This combines both the cable twist from right to left and cable twist from left to right, to produce a fabric with a completely different look although the methods used are exactly the same. Cast on and work the first 8 rows as given for cable twist from right to left.

9th row As 1st.

10th row As 2nd.

Rep 9th and 10th rows twice more.

15th row P9, C6B, P9.

16th row As 10th.

Rep 9th and 10th rows twice more. Cast off.

This sample shows the same 3 stitches being moved on each twist.

Panels of cable twist from right to left

This pattern is made up of panels of 4 knitted stitches with one purl stitch between each panel, twisted from right to left on different rows to give a diagonal appearance. Cast on 31 stitches.

1st row P1, *K4, P1, rep from * to end.

2nd row K1, *P4, K1, rep from * to end.

3rd row P1, *K4, P1, sl next 2 sts on to cable needle and hold at front of work, K next 2 sts from left hand needle then K2 sts from cable needle — called C4F —, P1, rep from * to end.

4th row As 2nd.

Rep 1st and 2nd rows once more.

7th row P1, *C4F, P1, K4, P1, rep from * to end.

8th row As 2nd.

These 8 rows form the pattern. Repeat pattern rows 3 times more. Cast off.

This sample shows that the cable twist on every 4th row gives a very close, tight, rope look, whereas twisting on every 8th or 12th row gives a much softer look.

Cable variations

Based on combinations of the simple cable twists given before, the patterns which can be produced are numerous. All the variations given here can be worked as all-over patterns or as separate panels against a purl background.
Try incorporating single plaited cable as an all-over pattern on a plain jersey design, or use a panel of link cables to highlight the front and centre of the sleeves on a basic cardigan. Another simple alternative would be to work two samples of honeycomb cable and use these as patch pockets on a stocking stitch cardigan, using the reverse side, or purl side as the right side of the cardigan fabric.

Link cable

The cable pattern is worked over 12 knitted stitches against a purl background. For this sample cast on 24 stitches.
1st row P6, K12, P6.
2nd row K6, P12, K6.
Rep 1st and 2nd rows twice more.
7th row P6, sl next 3 sts on to cable needle and hold at back of work, K next 3 sts from left hand needle then K3 sts from cable needle — called C6B —, sl next 3 sts on to cable needle and hold at front of work, K next 3 sts from left hand needle then K3 sts from cable needle — called C6F —, P6.
8th row as 2nd.
These 8 rows form the pattern. Repeat pattern rows twice more. Cast off.
This pattern gives the appearance of chain links, each link coming upwards out of the one below.

Inverted link cable

Cast on and work the first 6 rows as given for link cable.
7th row P6, C6F, C6B, P6.
8th row As 2nd.
These 8 rows form the pattern. Repeat pattern rows twice more. Cast off.
This pattern has the reverse appearance of link cables with each link joining and passing under the link above.

Honeycomb cable

This pattern combines the working methods of link cable and inverted link cable. For this sample cast on 24 stitches.
1st row P6, K12, P6.
2nd row K6, P12, K6.

Rep 1st and 2nd rows once more.
5th row P6, C6B, C6F, P6.
6th row As 2nd.
Rep 1st and 2nd rows twice more.
11th row P6, C6F, C6B, P6.

12th row As 2nd.
These 12 rows form the pattern. Repeat pattern rows twice more. Cast off.
This pattern forms a cable which appears to be superimposed on the fabric beneath.

Single plaited cable
This pattern is achieved by dividing the groups of stitches which are to be cabled into three sections instead of two and cabling each group alternately. For this sample cast on 30 stitches.
1st row P3, *K6, P3, rep from * to end.
2nd row K3, *P6, K3, rep from * to end.
3rd row P3, *sl next 2 sts on to cable needle and hold at back of work, K next 2 sts from left hand needle then K2 from cable needle — called C4B —, K2, P3, rep from * to end.
4th row As 2nd.
5th row P3, *K2, sl next 2 sts on to cable needle and hold at front of work, K next 2 sts from left hand needle then K2 from cable needle — called C4F —, P3, rep from * to end.
6th row As 2nd.
The 3rd to 6th rows form the pattern. Repeat pattern rows 6 times more. Cast off.

Double plaited cable
This pattern is even more textured than single plaited cable and is worked over 18 knitted stitches against a purl background. For this sample cast on 30 sts.
1st row P6, K18, P6.
2nd row K6, P18, K6.
3rd row P6, (C6B) 3 times, P6.
4th row As 2nd.
Rep 1st and 2nd rows once more.
7th row P6, K3, (C6F) twice, K3, P6.
8th row As 2nd.

These 8 rows form the pattern. Repeat pattern rows twice more. Cast off.

Cable waves
Cable patterns have a completely different appearance when the stitches being moved are worked in knitting against a knitted background, instead of a purl fabric. For this sample cast on 24 stitches.
1st row K to end.
2nd and every alt row P to end.
3rd row *C6F, K6, rep from * to end.
5th row K to end.
7th row *K6, C6B, rep from * to end.
9th row K to end.
10th row As 2nd.
Rows 3 to 10 form the pattern. Repeat pattern rows twice more. Cast off.

Cables, bobbles and crossed stitches

The skilful and imaginative use of such patterns as cables, bobbles and crossed stitches, form the basis for a range of intricate and densely textured fabrics referred to as 'Aran' patterns. Most of the traditional stitches, with their highly evocative names, were originated in the remote Aran islands and derived their inspiration from the daily life of the islanders. The rocks are depicted by chunky bobble stitches, the cliff paths by zig-zag patterns, whilst the fishermen's ropes inspire a vast number of cable variations. The wealth of the sea around the islands, religious symbols and the ups and downs of married life all play a part in the formation of a rich tapestry of patterns, unique in knitting.

The Irish name for the thick, homespun yarn used for Aran knitting is 'bainin', which literally means 'natural'. These traditional stitches show to their best advantage in this light-coloured yarn but many vivid colours are now used with these stitches, to make fashion garments.

Practise the samples given here, using a Double Knitting yarn and No. 4mm (8) needles, to form separate squares or panels, which can then be joined together to form cushions, afghans or even bedspreads.

If you knit these samples you can join them together as a random patchwork, or knit a 'story' picture using the symbolic meaning of the stitches, so there is no need to regard these practice samplers as a waste.

Ladder of life

This simple design depicts man's eternal desire to climb upwards, the purl ridges forming the rungs of the ladder. Cast on a number of stitches divisible by 6 + 1.

1st row (RS) P1, *K5, P1, rep from * to end.
2nd row K1, *P5, K1, rep from * to end.
3rd row P to end.
4th row As 2nd.
These 4 rows form the pattern.

Lobster claw stitch

This represents the bounty of the sea. Cast on a number of stitches divisible by 9.

1st row (RS) *P1, K7, P1, rep from * to end.
2nd row *K1, P7, K1, rep from * to end.
3rd row *P1, sl next 2 sts on to cable needle and hold at back of work, K1 from left hand needle then K2 from cable needle, K1 from left hand needle, sl next st on to cable needle and hold at front of work, K2 from left hand needle then K1 from cable needle, P1, rep from * to end.
4th row As 2nd.
These 4 rows form the pattern.

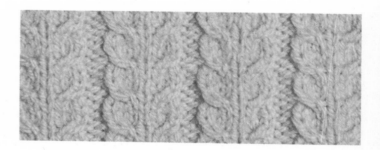

Tree of life

Narrow lines of travelling stitches branching out from a central stem form the basis for this traditional pattern. Cast on a number of stitches divisible by 15.

1st row (RS) *P7, K1, P7, rep from * to end.
2nd row *K7, P1, K7, rep from * to end.
3rd row *P5, sl next st on to cable needle and hold at back of work, K1 from left hand needle then P1 from cable needle — called C2B —, K1 from left hand needle, sl next st on to cable needle and hold at front of work, P1 from left hand needle then K1 from cable needle — called C2F —, P5, rep from * to end.
4th row *K5, sl 1 P-wise keeping yarn at front of work, K1, P1, K1, sl 1, K5, rep from * to end.
5th row *P4, C2B, P1, K1, P1, C2F, P4, rep from * to end.
6th row *K4, sl 1, K2, P1, K2, sl 1, K4, rep from * to end.
7th row *P3, C2B, P2, K1, P2, C2F, P3, rep

from * to end.
8th row *K3, sl 1, K3, P1, K3, sl 1, K3, rep from * to end.
9th row *P2, C2B, P3, K1, P3, C2F, P2, rep from * to end.
10th row *K2, sl 1, K4, P1, K4, sl 1, K2, rep from * to end.
These 10 rows form the pattern.

Aran plaited cable
This simple cable depicts the interweaving of family life. Cast on a number of stitches divisible by 12.
1st row (WS) *K2, P8, K2, rep from * to end.
2nd row *P2, (sl next 2 sts on to cable needle and hold at back of work, K2 from left hand needle then K2 from cable needle) twice, P2, rep from * to end.
3rd row As 1st.
4th row *P2, K2, sl next 2 sts on to cable needle and hold at front of work, K2 from left hand needle then K2 from cable needle, K2, P2, rep from * to end.
These 4 rows form the pattern.

Aran diamond and bobble cable
The small diamond outlined with knitted stitches represents the small, walled fields of Ireland and the bobble depicts the stony nature of the ground. Cast on a number of stitches divisible by 17.
1st row (WS) *K6, P2, K1, P2, K6, rep from * to end.
2nd row *P6, sl next 3 sts on to cable needle and hold at back of work, K2 from left hand needle,

sl P1 from end of cable needle back on to left hand needle and P1 then K2 from cable needle, P6, rep from * to end.
3rd row As 1st.

4th row *P5, sl next st on to cable needle and hold at back of work, K2 from left hand needle then P1 from cable needle — called C3B —, K1, sl next 2 sts on to cable needle and hold at front of work, P1 from left hand needle then K2 from cable needle — called C3F —, P5, rep from * to end.
5th and every alt row K all K sts and P all P sts.
6th row *P4, C3B, K1, P1, K1, C3F, P4, rep from * to end.
8th row *P3, C3B, (K1, P1) twice, K1, C3F, P3, rep from * to end.
10th row *P2, C3B, (K1, P1) 3 times, K1, C3F, P2, rep from * to end.
12th row *P2, C3F, (P1, K1) 3 times, P1, C3B, P2, rep from * to end.
14th row *P3, C3F, (P1, K1) twice, P1, C3B, P3, rep from * to end.
16th row *P4, C3F, P1, K1, P1, C3B, P4, rep from * to end.
18th row *P5, C3F, P1, C3B, P5, rep from * to end.
20th row As 2nd.
22nd row *P5, C3B, P1, C3F, P5, rep from * to end.
24th row *P4, C3B, P3, C3F, P4, rep from * to end.
26th row *P4, K2, P2, (K1, yfwd to make one st, K1, yfwd, K1) all into next st, turn and P5, turn and K5, turn and P2 tog, P1, P2 tog, turn and sl 1, K2 tog, psso — called B1 —, P2, K2, P4, rep from * to end.
28th row *P4, C3F, P3, C3B, P4, rep from * to end.
30th row As 18th.
These 30 rows form the pattern.

Cables in rounds

Cable patterns are just as easy to work in rounds as in rows. Unless otherwise stated in a pattern, the cable twists are worked on the right side of the fabric and as the right side of the work is always facing you when knitting in rounds. it is quite a simple matter to combine both of these techniques.

This jaunty little hat has been specially designed so that the cable panels can be worked in any one of three variations. This will help you master the method of working cable stitches — at the same time resulting in a snug, warm, fashion extra.

Size
To fit the average head

Tension
22 sts and 30 rows to 10cm (*3.9in*) over st st worked on No. 4½mm (*7*) needles

Materials
3 × 25 grm balls of any Double Knitting quality
One Set of 4 No. 5mm (*6*) needles pointed at both ends
One set of 4 No. 4½mm (*7*) needles pointed at both ends
One cable needle

Hat
Using set of 4 No. 5mm (*6*) needles cast on 96 sts and arrange on 3 needles.
1st round *P2, K2, rep from * to end.
Rep this round for 10cm (*4in*), to form turned-back brim. Change to set of 4 No. 4½mm (*7*) needles.
Commence patt.

Cable patt 1
1st round *P2, K6, rep from * to end.
2nd round As 1st.
3rd round As 1st.
4th round *P2, sl next 3 sts on to cable needle and hold at front of work, K next 3 sts from left hand needle then K3 from cable needle — called C6F —, rep from * to end.
These 4 rounds form the patt.

Cable patt 2
1st round *P2, K6, rep from * to end.
2nd round As 1st.
3rd round As 1st.
4th round *P2, sl next 3 sts on to cable needle and hold at front of work, K next 3 sts from left hand needle then K3 from cable needle — called C6F —, rep from * to end.
5th round As 1st.
6th round As 1st.
7th round As 1st.
8th round *P2, sl next 3 sts on to cable needle and hold at back of work, K next 3 sts from left hand needle then K3 from cable needle—called C6B—, rep from * to end.
These 8 rows form the patt.

Cable patt 3
1st round *P2, K6, rep from * to end.
2nd round As 1st.
3rd round As 1st.
4th round *P2, sl next 2 sts on to cable needle and hold at back of work, K next 2 sts from left hand needle then K2 from cable needle—called C4B —, K2, rep from * to end.
5th round As 1st.
6th round As 1st.
7th round As 1st.
8th round *P2, K2, sl next 2 sts on to cable needle and hold at front of work, K next 2 sts from left hand needle, then K2 from cable needle—C4F —, rep from * to end.
These 8 rounds form the patt.
Cont in patt as required until work measures 20cm (*8in*) from beg of patt, ending with a 4th or 8th patt round.

Shape top
Next round (dec round) *P2, sl 1, K1, psso, K2, K2 tog, rep from * to end. 72 sts.
Next round *P2, K4, rep from * to end.
Next round *P2, sl 1, K1, psso, K2 tog, rep from * to end. 48 sts.
Next round *P2, K2, rep from * to end.
Next round *P2 tog, K2 tog, rep from * to end. 24 sts.
Next round *P1, K1, rep from * to end.
Next round *Sl 1, K1, psso, rep from * to end. 12 sts.
Break off yarn, thread through rem sts, draw up and fasten off.

To make up
Pressing on WS is required, omitting ribbing and taking care not to flatten patt. Turn RS out.
Fold brim in half to outside then fold back again to form double brim.

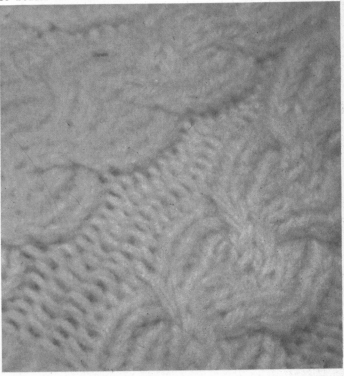

Aran design collection

Poncho

The variety and complexity of Aran stitches which may be formed give such scope for textured patterns that it is sometimes difficult to know where to begin a design and how best to combine these stitches to produce the most effective fabric. If each stitch is run on into the next, all definition will be lost and none of the stitches will show to their best advantage. Because these stitches nearly always have a raised texture, their beauty is enhanced if they are worked against a purled background. Similarly, if each panel of stitches is enclosed with a rope of twisted stitches and alternated with panels of either purl or moss stitches, each separate Aran panel stands out without detracting in any way from the next panel. The poncho design given here uses these techniques to full effect. It is made from two simple sections and the size can easily be adjusted by amending the number of stitches in each purl panel.

Poncho
Size
Approx 89cm (*35in*) square, excluding fringe

Tension
18 sts and 24 rows to 10cm (*3.9in*) over st st worked on No. 4½mm (*7*) needles

Materials
17 × 50grm balls Blarney Bainin Wool
One pair No. 4½mm (*7*) needles
One pair No. 4mm (*8*) needles
One set of 4 No. 3¾mm (*9*) needles pointed at both ends
One No. 4½mm (*7*) circular Twin Pin
One No. 4mm (*8*) circular Twin Pin
One cable needle

Poncho first section
Using No. 4mm (*8*) circular Twin Pin cast on 146 sts.
Next row (inc row) K3, pick up loop lying between needles and P tbl — called M1 —, K2, M1, *(K2, M1) twice, (K2, K into front and back of next st — called Kfb —) twice, K3, (M1, K2) twice, *, ** (M1, K2) twice, (P1, M1, P1, P into front and back of next st — called Pfb —, P1, M1, P1, K2) twice, M1, K2, M1, **, ***K2, Pfb, K2, Kfb, K3, Pfb, K1, Pfb, K2, Kfb, K3, Pfb, K2, ***, rep from ** to **, then from *** to *** then from ** to ** again, then rep from * to * once more, M1, K2, M1, K3. 204 sts.
Change to No. 4½mm (*7*) circular Twin Pin. Commence patt.
1st row K2, P1, K1 tbl, P2, K1 tbl, *P2, sl next st on to cable needle and hold at front of work, P1, then K1 tbl from cable needle—called T21—, P1, T2L, P9, sl next st on to cable needle and hold at back of work, K1 tbl, then P1 from cable needle—called T2R—, P1, T2R, P2, *, K1 tbl, P2, K1 tbl, **(P2, K8) twice, P2, K1 tbl, P2, K1 tbl, P2, K2, P3, into next st (K1, (yfwd, K1) twice, turn, these 5 sts, turn, K5, turn, P5, turn, sl 2nd, 3rd and 4th sts over first st, then K first and last st tog tbl—called MB—P3, sl next 3 sts on to cable needle and hold at back of work, K2, sl P st from cable needle on to left hand needle and hold cable needle at front of work, P1 from left hand needle, then K2 from cable needle—called Cr5—, P3, MB, P3, K2, P2, K1 tbl, P2, K1 tbl, **, rep from ** to ** once more, (P2, K8) twice, P2, K1 tbl, P2, K1 tbl, rep from * to * once more, K1 tbl, P2, K1 tbl, P1, K2.
2nd row K3, *P1 tbl, K2, P1 tbl, K3, P1 tbl, K2, P1 tbl, K9, P1 tbl, K2, P1 tbl, K3, *, P1 tbl, K2, P1 tbl, **(K2, P8) twice, K2, P1 tbl, K2, P1 tbl, K2, (P2, K7, P2, K1) twice, K1, P1 tbl, K2, P1 tbl, **, rep from ** to ** once more, (Ks, P8*) twice K2, rep from * to * once more, P1 tbl, K2, P1 tbl, K3.
3rd row K2, P1, *K1 tbl, P2, K1 tbl, P3, T2L, P1, T2L, P7, T2R, P1, T2R, P3, *, K1 tbl, P2, K1 tbl, **(P2, sl next 2 sts on to cable needle and hold at back of work, K2, then K2 from cable needle—called C4B—, sl next 2 sts on to cable needle and hold at front of work, K2, then K2 from cable needle—called C2F—) twice, P2, K1 tbl, P2, K1 tbl, P2, (sl next 2 sts on to cable needle and hold at front of work, P1, then K2 from cable needle—called C3L—, P5, sl next st on to cable needle and hold at back of work, K2, then P1 from cable needle—called C3R—, P1) twice, P1, K1 tbl, P2,

5th row K2, P1, K1 tbl, *P2, K1 tbl, P4, T2L, P1, T2L, P5, T2R, P1, T2R, P4, *, K1 tbl, P2, K1 tbl, **(P2, K8) twice, P2, K1 tbl, P2, K1 tbl, (P3, C3L, P3, C3R) twice, P3, K1 tbl, P2, K1 tbl, **, rep from ** to ** once more, (P2, K8) twice, P2, K1 tbl, rep from * to * once more, K1 tbl, P2, K1 tbl, P1,K2.

6th row K3,P1 tbl, *K2, P1 tbl, (K5, P1 tbl, K2, P1 tbl) twice, K5, *, P1 tbl, K2, P1 tbl, **(K2, P8) twice, K2, P1 tbl, K2, P1 tbl, K4, P2, K3, P2, K5, P2, K3, P2, K4, P1 tbl, K2, P1 tbl, **, rep from ** to ** once more, (K2, P8) twice, K2, P1 tbl, rep from * to * once more, P1 tbl, K2, P1 tbl, K3.

7th row K2, P1, K1 tbl, *P2, K1 tbl, P5, T2L, P1, T2L, P3, T2R, P1, T2R, P5, *, K1 tbl, P2, K1 tbl, **(P2, C4B, C4F) twice, P2, K1 tbl, P2, K1 tbl, P4, C3L, P1, C3R, P5, C3L, P1, C3R, P4, K1 tbl, P2, K1 tbl, **, rep from ** to ** once more, (P2, C4B, C4F) twice, P2, K1 tbl, rep from * to * once more, K1 tbl, P2, K1 tbl, P1, K2.

8th row K3, P1 tbl, *K2, P1 tbl, K6, P1 tbl, K2, P1 tbl, K3, P1 tbl, K2, P1 tbl, K6, *, P1 tbl, K2, P1 tbl, **(K2, P8) twice, K2, P1 tbl, K2, P1 tbl, K5, P2, K1, P2, K7, P2, K1, P2, K5, P1 tbl, K2, P1 tbl, **, rep from ** to ** once more, (K2, P8) twice, K2, P1 tbl, rep from * to * once more, P1 tbl, K2, P1 tbl, K3.

9th row K2, P1, K1 tbl, *P2, K1 tbl, P5, T2R, P1, T2R, P3, T2L, P1, T2L, P5, *, K1 tbl, P2, K1 tbl, **(P2, K8) twice, P2, K1 tbl, P2, K1 tbl, P5, Cr5, P3, MB, P3, Cr5, P5, K1 tbl, P2 K1 tbl, **, rep from ** to ** once more, (P2, K8) twice, P2, K1 tbl, rep from * to * once more, K1 tbl, P2, K1 tbl, P1, K2.

10th row K3, P1 tbl, *K2, P1 tbl, (K5, P1 tbl, K2, P1 tbl) twice, K5, *, P1 tbl, K2, P1 tbl, **(K2, P8) twice, K2, P1 tbl, K2, P1 tbl, K5, P2, K1, P2, K7, P2, K1, P2, K5, P1 tbl, K2, P1 tbl, **, rep from ** to ** once more, (K2, P8) twice, K2, P1 tbl, rep from * to * once more, P1 tbl, K2, P1 tbl, K3.

11th row K2, P1, K1 tbl, *P2, K1 tbl, P4, T2R, P1, T2R, P5, T2L, P1, T2L, P4, *, K1 tbl, P2, K1 tbl, **(P2, C4F, C4B) twice, P2, K1 tbl, P2, K1 tbl, P4, C3R, P1, C3L, P5, C3R, P1, C3L, P4, K1 tbl, P2, K1 tbl, **, rep from ** to ** once more, (P2, C4F, C4B) twice, P2, K1 tbl, rep from * to * once more, K1 tbl, P2, K1 tbl, P1, K2.

12th row K3, P1 tbl, *K2, P1 tbl, K4, P1 tbl, K2, P1 tbl, K7, P1 tbl, K2, P1 tbl, K4, *, P1 tbl, K2, P1 tbl, **(K2, P8) twice, K2, P1 tbl, K2, P1 tbl, K4, P2, K3, P2, K5, P2, K3, P2, K4, P1 tbl, K2, P1 tbl, **, rep from ** to ** once more, (K2, P8) twice, K2, P1 tbl, rep from * to * once more, P1 tbl, K2, P1 tbl, K3.

13th row K2, P1, K1 tbl, *P2, K1 tbl, P3, T2R,

K1 tbl, **, rep from ** to ** once more, (P2, C4B, C4F) twice, P2, rep from * to * once more, K1 tbl, P2, K1 tbl, P1, K2.

4th row K3, P1 tbl, K2, *P1 tbl, K4, P1 tbl, K2, P1 tbl, K7, P1 tbl, K2, P1 tbl, K4, *, P1 tbl, K2, P1 tbl, **(K2, P8*) twice, K2, P1 tbl, K2, P1 tbl, (K3, P2, K5, P2) twice, K3, P1 tbl, K2, P1 tbl, **, rep from ** to ** once more, (K2, P8) twice, K2, P1 tbl, K2, rep from * to * once more, P1 tbl, K2, P1 tbl, K3.

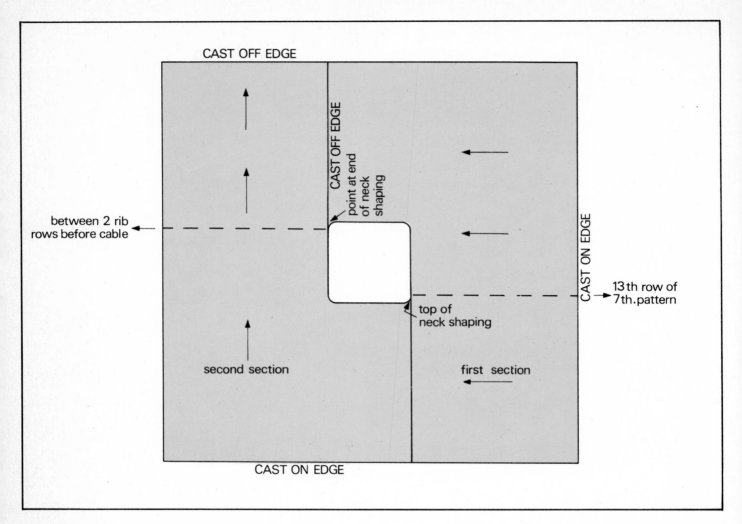

CAST OFF EDGE

CAST OFF EDGE

point at end of neck shaping

between 2 rib rows before cable

CAST ON EDGE

13th row of 7th. pattern

top of neck shaping

second section

first section

CAST ON EDGE

P1, T2R, P7, T2L, P1, T2L, P3, *, K1 tbl, P2, K1 tbl, **(P2, K8) twice, P2, K1 tbl, P2, K1 tbl, (P3, C3R, P3, C3L) twice, P3, K1 tbl, P2, K1 tbl, **, rep from ** to ** once more, (P2, K8) twice, P2, K1 tbl, rep from * to * once more, K1 tbl, P2, K1 tbl, P1, K2.

14th row K3, P1 tbl, *K2, P1 tbl, K3, P1 tbl, K2, P1 tbl, K9, P1 tbl, K2, P1 tbl, K3, *, P1 tbl, K2, P1 tbl, **(K2, P8) twice, K2, P1 tbl, K2, P1 tbl, (K3, P2, K5, P2) twice, K3, P1 tbl, K2, P1 tbl, **, rep from ** to ** once more, (K2, P8) twice, K2, P1 tbl, rep from * to * once more, P1 tbl, K2, P1 tbl, K3.

15th row K2, P1, K1 tbl, *P2, K1 tbl, P2, T2R, P1, T2R, P9, T2L, P1, T2L, P2, *, K1 tbl, P2, K1 tbl, **(P2, C4F, C4B) twice, P2, K1 tbl, P2, K1 tbl, P2, (C3R, P5, C3L, P1) twice, P1, K1 tbl, P2, K1 tbl, **, rep from ** to ** once more, (P2, C4F, C4B) twice, P2, K1 tbl, rep from * to * once more, K1 tbl, P2, K1 tbl, P1, K2.

16th row K3, P1 tbl, *K2, P1 tbl, (K2, P1 tbl) twice, K11 (P1 tbl, K2) twice, *, P1 tbl, K2, P1 tbl, ** (K2, P8) twice, K2, P1 tbl, K2, P1 tbl, K2, (P2, K7, P2, K1) twice, K1, P1 tbl, K2, P1 tbl,

**, rep from ** to ** once more, (K2, P8) twice, K2, P1 tbl, rep from * to * once more, P1 tbl, K2, P1 tbl, K3.

These 16 rows form patt. Cont in patt until 8th row of 6th patt has been completed.

Shape neck

Next row Patt 93 sts, *(K2 tog, K1) twice, K2 tog, P2, (K2 tog, K1) twice, K2 tog, *, (P1, K2 tog) twice, **P5, K2 tog, P1, K2 tog, (P1, P2 tog) twice, (P1, K2 tog) twice, P5, **, (K2 tog tbl, P1) twice, rep from * to * once more, (P1, K2 tog) twice, P2, P2 tog, (P1, K2 tog) twice, P3, (K2 tog tbl, P1) twice, P2 tog, K2 tog tbl, P1, K2 tog tbl, K2. 172 sts.

Next row Cast off 79 sts, patt to end. 93 sts.

Next row Patt to last 2 sts, P2 tog.

Keeping patt correct, cont dec one st at beg of next and every foll alt row 5 times in all. Work 8 rows without shaping. Inc one st at end of next and every alt row 6 times in all. 93 sts.

Next row K2, K2 tog, P1, K2 tog, P2, P2 tog, (P1, K2 tog tbl) twice, P3, (K2 tog, P1) twice, P2 tog, P2, (K2 tog tbl, P1) twice, rep from * to * of 1st shaping row, (P1, K2 tog) twice, rep from ** to

** of 1st shaping row, patt to end. 69 sts.
Cast off loosely.

Second section
Using No. 4mm (8) needles cast on 83 sts. K 4 rows
g st.
Next row (inc row) K3, M1, K2, M1, rep from *
to * of inc row in first section, then from ** to **
in same row, then from *** to *** in same row,
then from ** to ** again, omitting M1 at end of
row. 116 sts.
Change to No. 4½mm (7) needles. Commence patt.
1st row K1, P1, K1 tbl, (P2, K8) twice, P2, K1 tbl,
P2, K1 tbl, P2, K2, P3, MB, P3, Cr5, P3, MB, P3,
K2, P2, K1 tbl, P2, K1 tbl, (P2, K8) twice, P2,
K1 tbl, P2, K1 tbl, P2, T2L, P1, T2L, P9, T2R, P1,
T2R, P2, K1 tbl, P2, K1 tbl, P1, K2.
2nd row K3, P1 tbl, K2, P1 tbl, patt as now set
to last 3 sts, P1 tbl, K2.
Cont in patt as now set until 8th row of 6th patt
has been completed.
Shape neck
1st row K1, P1, K1 tbl, P2, (K2 tog, K1) twice,
K2 tog, P2, (K2 tog, K1) twice, K2 tog, patt to end.
2nd row Patt 93 sts and leave these sts on a holder,
cast off 12 sts, patt to end. 5 sts.
Dec one st at neck edge on foll 3 alt rows. Cast off.
With RS of work facing, rejoin yarn to rem sts at
neck edge, cont in patt dec one st at neck edge on
foll 3 alt rows. 90 sts. Cont without shaping until
13th patt rep has been completed. Change to
No. 4mm (8) needles.
Next row K2, (K2 tog, K2, K2 tog, K1) 12
times, K2 tog, K2. 65 sts.
K3 rows g st. Cast off.

To make up
Join both sections as shown in diagram, noting
position of top of neck shaping on second section
and point at end of neck shaping on first section.
Press seams on wrong side under a damp cloth
with a warm iron.
Neckband Using set of 4 No. 3¾mm (9) needles,
K up 104 sts all round neck edge. Work 5 rounds
K1, P1 rib. Cast off in rib, working K2 tog at
each corner.
Fringe Cut yarn into lengths of 25.5cm (10in).
Using 3 strands folded in half, draw centre of
threads through edge of poncho and knot. Rep at
1.5cm (½in) intervals all round outer edge.
This versatile poncho can be worn on almost any
occasion. It makes the ideal practice ground for
your aran stitches. You will be pleasantly surprised
at how quickly your knitting grows and once you
master the more intricate aran variations you will
be able to follow almost any pattern of your choice,
and now to move on to aran shaping.

Camisole top

Aran shaping
Where an Aran panel is combined with alternate
panels of purl or moss stitches, it is simple to
make provision for any shaping. Because Aran
stitches are rather complex, it is not advisable to
try and combine them with any increasing or
decreasing and most designs take this into account.
The number of stitches required, say, for a raglan
armhole and sleeve top shaping are carefully
calculated to ensure that the correct number of
stitches are decreased in a plain panel, without
interfering with the Aran panels.
The variety of Aran designs available is sometimes

restricted by this problem of shaping. This can be overcome, however, by the skilful use of shaping in each alternate plain panel and by the careful choice of a basic stitch, such as garter stitch or ribbing, to complete the shaped sections. The camisole top shown here perfectly illustrates these techniques.

Camisole top
Sizes
To fit 81.5[86.5:,91.5]cm (*32[34:36]in*) bust
Length to shoulder 47[49:51]cm (*18[19¼:20]in*)
The figures in brackets [] refer to the 86.5 (*34*) and 91.5cm (*36in*) sizes respectively

Tension
32 sts and 40 rows to 10cm (*3.9in*) over rev st st worked on No. 3mm (*11*) needles

Materials
8 × 25 grm balls Little Poppet by 3 Suisse
One pair No. 3mm (*11*) needles
One No. 3mm (*11*) circular Twin Pin
One No. 2¾mm (*12*) circular Twin Pin
7 buttons

Camisole fronts and back
Using No. 2¾mm (*12*) circular Twin Pin cast on 237[253:269] sts and work in one piece, beg at lower edge.
1st row K1, *P1, K1, rep from * to end.
2nd row P1, *K1, P1, rep from * to end.
Rep last 2 rows 3 times more, then 1st row once more.
Next row P to end.
Next row P to end to form hemline.
Base row Cast on 7 sts for right front band, turn, K8, *P2, K15, P2, K8[10:12], P2, K3, P1, K2, P1, K8, P2, K8[10:12], rep from * 3 times more, P2, K15, P2, K1, turn and cast on 7 sts for left front band. 251[267:283] sts.
Change to No. 3mm (*11*) circular Twin Pin.
Commence patt.
1st row (RS) K7, P1, *K 2nd st on left hand needle, then first st — called T2 —, P7, K1, P7, T2, P8[10:12], T2, P7, K 2nd st on left hand needle, then P first st — called C2R —, P1, C2R, P3, T2, P8[10:12], T2, P2, K2, P7, K2, P2, T2, P8[10:12], T2, P7, C2R, P1, C2R, P3, T2, P8[10:12], rep from * once more, T2, P7, K1, P7, T2, P1, K7.
2nd row K8, *P2, K7, P1, K7, P2, K8[10:12], P2, K4, P1, K2, P1, K7, P2, K8[10:12], P2, K2, P3, K5, P3, K2, P2, K8[10:12], P2, K4, P1, K2, P1, K7, P2, K8[10:12], rep from * once more, P2, K7, P1, K7, P2, K8.
3rd row K7, P1, *T2, P6, K1, P1, K1, P6, T2,
P8[10:12], T2, P6, C2R, P1, C2R, P4, T2, P8[10:12], T2, (P3, K3) twice, P3, T2, P8[10:12], T2, P6, C2R, P1, C2R, P4, T2, P8[10:12], rep from * once more, T2, P6, K1, P1, K1, P6, T2, P1, K7.
4th row K8, *P2, K6, P1, K1, P1, K6, P2, K8[10:12], P2, K5, P1, K2, P1, K6, P2, K8[10:12], P2, K4, P3, K1, P3, K4, P2, K8[10:12], P2, K5, P1, K2, P1, K6, P2, K8[10:12], rep from * once more, P2, K6, P1, K1, P1, K6, P2, K8.
5th row (buttonhole row) K2, K2 tog, (yrn) twice, sl 1, K1, psso, K1, P1, *T2, P5, (K1, P1) twice, K1, P5, T2, P8[10:12], T2, P5, C2R, P1, C2R, P5, T2, P8[10:12], T2, P5, K5, P5, T2, P8[10:12], T2, P5, C2R, P1, C2R, P5, T2, P8[10:12], rep from * once more, T2, P5, (K1, P1) twice, K1, P5, T2, P1, K7.
6th row K8, *P2, K5, (P1, K1) twice, P1, K5, P2, K8[10:12], P2, K6, P1, K2, P1, K5, P2, K8[10:12], P2, K6, P3, K6, P2, K8[10:12], P2, K6, P1, K2, P1, K5, P2, K8[10:12], rep from * once more, P2, K5, (P1, K1) twice, P1, K5, P2, K3, drop one loop of double loop to make long st and work K1, P1 into same st, K3.
Work 5 more buttonholes in same way with 18[20:22] rows between each buttonhole.
7th row K7, P1, *T2, P4, (K1, P1) 3 times, K1, P4, T2, P8[10:12], T2, P4, C2R, P1, C2R, P6, T2, P8[10:12], T2, P5, K5, P5, T2, P8[10:12], T2, P4, C2R, P1, C2R, P6, T2, P8[10:12], rep from * once more, T2, P4, (K1, P1) 3 times, K1, P4, T2, P1, K7.
8th row K8, *P2, K4, (P1, K1) 3 times, P1, K4, P2, K8[10:12], P2, K7, P1, K2, P1, K4, P2, K8[10:12], P2, K4, P3, K1, P3, K4, P2, K8[10:12], P2, K7, P1, K2, P1, K4, P2, K8[10:12], rep from * once more, P2, K4, (P1, K1) 3 times, P1, K4, P2, K8.
9th row K7, P1, *T2, P3, (K1, P1) 4 times, K1, P3, T2, P8[10:12], T2, P3, C2R, P1, C2R, P7, T2, P8[10:12], T2, (P3, K3) twice, P3, T2, P8[10:12], T2, P3, C2R, P1, C2R, P7, T2, P8[10:12], rep from * once more, T2, P3, (K1, P1) 4 times, K1, P3, T2, P1, K7.
10th row K8, *P2, K3, (P1, K1) 4 times, P1, K3, P2, K8[10:12], P2, K8, P1, K2, P1, K3, P2, K8[10:12], P2, K2, P3, K5, P3, K2, P2, K8[10:12], P2, K8, P1, K2, P1, K3, P2, K8[10:12], rep from * once more, P2, K3, (P1, K1) 4 times, P1, K3, P2, K8.
11th row K7, P1, *T2, P2, (K1, P1) 5 times, K1, P2, T2, P8[10:12], T2, P3, K1, P2, K1, P8, T2, P8[10:12], T2, P2, K2, P7, K2, P2, T2, P8[10:12], T2, P3, K1, P2, K1, P8, T2, P8[10:12], rep from * once more, T2, P2, (K1, P1) 5 times, K1, P2, T2, P1, K7.
12th row K8, *P2, K2, (P1, K1) 5 times, P1, K2, P2, K8[10:12], P2, K8, P1, K2, P1, K3, P2,

K8[10:12], P2, K15, P2, K8[10:12], P2, K8, P1, K2, P1, K3, P2, K8[10:12], rep from * once more, P2, K2, (P1, K1) 5 times, P1, K2, P2, K8.

13th row K7, P1, *T2, P3, (K1, P1) 4 times, K1, P3, T2, P8[10:12], T2, P3, P 2nd st on left hand needle, then K first st — called C2L —, P1, C2L, P7, T2, P8[10:12], T2, P6, K3, P6, T2, P8[10:12], T2, P3, C2L, P1, C2L, P7, T2, P8[10:12], rep from * once more, T2, P3, (K1, P1) 4 times, K1, P3, T2, P1, K7.

Shape waist

14th row K8, *P2, K3, (P1, K1) 4 times, P1, K3, P2, sl 1, K1, psso, K4[6:8], K2 tog, P2, K7, P1, K2, P1, K4, P2, sl 1, K1, psso, K4[6:8], K2 tog, P2, K5, P5, K5, P2, sl 1, K1, psso, K4[6:8], K2 tog, P2, K7, P1, K2, P1, K4, P2, sl 1, K1, psso, K4[6:8], K2 tog, rep from * once more, P2, K3, (P1, K1) 4 times, P1, K3, P2, K8. 235[251:267] sts.

15th row K7, P1, *T2, P4, (K1, P1) 3 times, K1, P4, T2, P6[8:10], T2, P4, C2L, P1, C2L, P6, T2, P6[8:10], T2, P4, K3, P1, K3, P4, T2, P6[8:10], T2, P4, C2L, P1, C2L, P6, T2, P6[8:10], rep from * once more, T2, P4, (K1, P1) 3 times, K1, P4, T2, P1, K7.

16th row K8, *P2, K4, (P1, K1) 3 times, P1, K4, P2, K6[8:10], P2, K6, P1, K2, P1, K5, P2,

K6[8:10], P2, (K3, P3) twice, K3, P2, K6[8:10], P2, K6, P1, K2, P1, K5, P2, K6[8:10], rep from * once more, P2, K4, (P1, K1) 3 times, P1, K4, P2, K8.

17th row K7, P1, *T2, P5, (K1, P1) twice, K1, P5, T2, P6[8:10], T2, P5, C2L, P1, C2L, P5, T2, P6[8:10], T2, P2, K3, P5, K3, P2, T2, P6[8:10], T2, P5, C2L, P1, C2L, P5, T2, P6[8:10], rep from * once more, T2, P5, (K1, P1) twice, K1, P5, T2, P1, K7.

18th row K8, *P2, K5, (P1, K1) twice, P1, K5, P2, K6[8:10], P2, K5, P1, K2, P1, K6, P2, K6[8:10], P2, K2, P2, K7, P2, K2, P2, K6[8:10], P2, K5, P1, K2, P1, K6, P2, K6[8:10], rep from * once more, P2, K5, (P1, K1) twice, P1, K5, P2, K8.

19th row K7, P1, *T2, P6, K1, P1, K1, P6, T2, P6[8:10], T2, P6, C2L, P1, C2L, P4, T2, P6[8:10], T2, P2, K3, P5, K3, P2, T2, P6[8:10], T2, P6, C2L, P1, C2L, P4, T2, P6[8:10], rep from * once more, T2, P6, K1, P1, K1, P6, T2, P1, K7.

20th row K8, *P2, K6, P1, K1, P1, K6, P2, sl 1, K1, psso, K2[4:6], K2 tog, P2, K4, P1, K2, P1, K7, P2, sl 1, K1, psso, K2[4:6], K2 tog, P2, (K3, P3) twice, K3, P2, sl 1, K1, psso, K2[4:6], K2 tog, P2, K4, P1, K2, P1, K7, P2, sl 1, K1, psso, K2[4:6], K2 tog, rep from * once more, P2, K6, P1, K1, P1, K6, P2, K8. 219[235:251] sts.

21st row K7, P1, *T2, P7, K1, P7, T2, P4[6:8], T2, P7, C2L, P1, C2L, P3, T2, P4[6:8], T2, P4, K3, P1, K3, P4, T2, P4[6:8], T2, P7, C2L, P1, C2L, P3, T2, P4[6:8], rep from * once more, T2, P7, K1, P7, T2, P1, K7.

22nd row K8, *P2, K7, P1, K7, P2, K4[6:8], P2, K3, P1, K2, P1, K8, P2, K4[6:8], P2, K5, P5, K5, P2, K4[6:8], P2, K3, P1, K2, P1, K8, P2, K4[6:8], rep from * once more, P2, K7, P1, K7, P2, K8.

23rd row K7, P1, *T2, P15, T2, P4[6:8], T2, P8, K1, P2, K1, P3, T2, P4[6:8], T2, P6, K3, P6, T2, P4[6:8], T2, P8, K1, P2, K1, P3, T2, P4[6:8], rep from * once more, T2, P15, T2, P1, K7.

24th row K8, *P2, K15, P2, K4[6:8], P2, K3, P1, K2, P1, K8, P2, K4[6:8], P2, K15, P2 K4[6:8], P2, K3, P1, K2, P1, K8, P2, K4[6:8], rep from * once more, P2, K15, P2, K8.

These 24 rows set patt for Aran panels with rev st st between each one. Cont in patt as now set, dec 2 sts as before within each rev st st panel on foll alt row. 203[219:235] sts. Cont in patt until work measures 11.5[12:12.5]cm ($4\frac{1}{2}[4\frac{3}{4}:5]in$) from hemline, ending with a RS row.

Next row K8, *P2, patt 15, P2, pick up loop lying between needles and K tbl — called M1 —, K2[4:6], M1, rep from * 7 times more, P2, patt 15, P2, K8.

Cont in patt, inc 2 sts as before within each rev st st panel on foll 20th row twice more. 251[267:283] sts. Cont in patt without shaping until work measures 28[29:30.5]cm (*11[11½:12]in*) from hemline, ending with a WS row.

Shape yoke
Next row K8, *K2 tog, K6, K2 tog, K7, K2 tog, K8[10:12], rep from * 7 times more, K2 tog, K6, K2 tog, K7, K2 tog, K8. 224[240:256] sts. Beg with a K row, cont in g st until work measures 30.5[31.5:33]cm (*12[12½:13]in*) from hemline, ending with a WS row.

Divide for armholes
Change to No. 3mm (*11*) needles.
Next row K55[58:61], turn and leave rem sts on holder.
Complete right front first.

Shape armhole
Cast off at beg of next and every foll alt row 2 sts 3 times and one st 3[4:5] times, *at the same time* work 7th buttonhole 18[20:22] rows above 6th buttonhole. K 2 rows, ending at front edge.

Shape neck
Cast off at beg of next and every foll alt row 23[24:25] sts once, 4 sts once, 2 sts 3 times and one st 3 times. 10[11:12] sts. Cont without shaping until work measures 47[49:51]cm (*18[19¼:20]in*) from hemline. Cast off.
With RS of work facing, rejoin yarn to back sts, cast off first 8[10:12] sts, K until there are 98[104:110] sts on right hand needle, turn and leave rem sts on holder for left front. Complete back first.

Shape armholes
Cast off 2 sts at beg of next 5 rows.

Shape back neck
Next row Cast off 2, K until there are 26[28:30] sts on right hand needle, cast off 34[36:38] sts for neck, K to end.
Dec one st at armhole edge on every alt row 3[4:5] times in all, *at the same time* cast off at neck edge on every alt row 4 sts once, 2 sts 3 times and one st 3 times. 10[11:12] sts. Cont without shaping until work measures 47[49:51]cm (*18[19¼:20]in*) from hemline. Cast off.
With WS of work facing, rejoin yarn to rem back sts and complete as given for first side, reversing shaping.
With RS of work facing, rejoin yarn to rem left front sts, cast off 8[10:12] sts, K to end. 55[58:61] sts. Complete to match right front, reversing shaping and omitting buttonhole.

To make up
Press under a damp cloth with a warm iron. Join shoulder seams. Turn hem to WS at lower edge and sl st down. Press seams. Sew on buttons.

Sportsman's jersey

Sizes
To fit 91.5[96.5:101.5:106.5]cm (*36[38:40:42]in*) chest
Length to center back of neck excluding neckband, 70.5[71:71.5:72.5]cm (*27¾[28:28¼:28½]in*)
Sleeve seam, 48.5[48.5:49.5:49.5]cm (*19[19:19½:19½]in*)
The figures in brackets[] refer to the 96.5 (*38*), 101.5 (*40*) and 106.5cm (*42in*) sizes respectively

Tension
24 sts and 30 rows to 10cm (*3.9in*) over rice st worked on No. 4mm (*8*) needles

Materials
17[18:18:19] × 40gr balls Grovenor by 3 Suisse Sports Yarn
One pair No. 4mm (*8*) needles
One pair No 3¼mm (*10*) needles   Cable needle

Back
Using No. 3¼mm (*10*) needles cast on 106[114:118:126] sts.
1st and 2nd sizes only
1st row (RS) K2, *P2, K2, rep from * to end.
2nd row P2, *K2, P2, rep from * to end.
Rep these 2 rows 8 times more, then 1st row once more.
3rd and 4th sizes only
1st row (RS) P2, *K2, P2, rep from * to end.
2nd row K2, *P2, K2, rep from * to end.
Rep these 2 rows 8 times more, then 1st row once more.
All sizes
Next row (inc row) (K3[5:6:8] sts, K into front and back of next st — called Kfb —) twice, K4, *P2, P into front and back of next st — called Pfb —, P3, K2, P2, Pfb, P4, Pfb, P2, K2, P2, Pfb, P3, *, K2, (P4, Pfb) 4 times, P6, K2, rep from * to * once more, (K3[5:6:8] sts, Kfb) twice, K4. 122[130:134:142] sts.
Change to No. 4mm (*8*) needles. Commence patt.
1st row (RS) (K1 tbl, P1) 7[9:10:12] times, *K7, P2, K12, P2, K7, *, P2, work honeycomb patt over next 30 sts by (sl next 2 sts on to cable needle and hold at back of work, K1 then K2 from cable needle — called Tr —, sl next st on to cable needle and hold at front of work, K2 then K1

18

from cable needle — called TL —) 5 times, P2, rep from * to * once more, (P1, K1 tbl) 7[9:10:12] times.

2nd and every alt row K14[18:20:24] sts, *P7, K2, P12, K2, P7, *, K2, P30, K2, rep from * to * once more, K14[18:20:24] sts.

Cont keeping 14[18:20:24] sts in rice st at each end as given in last 2 rows.

3rd row Rice st 14[18:20:24], *Tr, K1, TL, P2, K12, P2, Tr, K1, TL, *, P2, (TL, Tr) 5 times, P2, rep from * to * once more, rice st 14[18:20:24].

5th row Rice st 14[18:20:24], *K7, P2, sl next 3 sts on to cable needle and hold at back of work, K3 then K3 from cable needle — called C6B —, sl next 3 sts on to cable needle and hold at front of work, K3 then K3 from cable needle — called C6F —, P2, K7, *, P2, (Tr, TL) 5 times, P2, rep from * to * once more, rice st 14[18:20:24].

7th row As 3rd.

9th row As 1st

11th row Rice st 14[18:20:24], *Tr, K1, TL, P2, C6B, C6F, P2, Tr, K1, TL, *, P2, (TL, Tr) 5 times, P2, rep from * to * once more, rice st 14[18:20:24].

13th row As 1st.

15th row As 3rd.

17th row Rice st 14[18:20:24], *K7, P2, C6F, C6B, P2, K7, *, P2, (Tr, TL) 5 times, P2, rep from * to * once more, rice st 14[18:20:24].

19th row As 3rd.

21st row As 1st.

23rd row Rice st 14[18:20:24], *Tr, K1, TL, P2, C6F, C6B, P2, Tr, K1, TL, *, P2, (TL, Tr) 5 times, P2, rep from * to * once more, rice st 14[18:20:24].

24th row As 2nd.

These 24 rows form patt. Cont in patt, inc 1[0:1:0] st at each end of row when work measures 18cm (*7in*) from beg. Cont in patt keeping 15[18:21:24] sts in rice st at each end until work measures 48.5cm (*19in*) from beg, ending with a WS row and noting which patt row has just been completed.

Shape raglans

**Keeping patt correct throughout, cast off 4 sts at beg of next 2 rows. Dec one st at each end of next and foll 24 alt rows, ending with a WS row. Dec one st at each end of next 2 rows then work 1 row without shaping. Rep last 3 rows 3 times more. Dec one st at each end of next 2[4:6:8] rows. **. Cast off rem 46[48:50:52] sts for centre back neck.

Front

Work as given for back until front measures 16 rows less than back to raglan shaping, ending with a WS row.

Divide for front and shape raglan

1st row Rice st 15[18:21:24], patt 30 sts, P2, work 12 sts in honeycomb patt, K2, turn and leave rem sts on holder.

Complete left front on these 61[64:67:70] sts. Work 3 rows without shaping then dec one st at neck edge on next row. Rep last 4 rows twice more. Work 3 rows without shaping, ending at side edge.

17th row Cast off 4 sts, patt to last 2 sts, K2 tog.

18th row Patt to end. ***

19th row Work in patt, dec one st at raglan edge.

20th row Patt to end.

21st row Work in patt, dec one st at raglan and neck edge.

22nd row Patt to end.

Rep 19th to 22nd rows 11 times more. 17[20:23:26] sts. Dec one st at neck and raglan edge on next row, dec one st at raglan edge only on foll row then work 1 row without shaping. Rep last 3 rows 3 times more. 5[8:11:14] sts.

1st size only

Dec one st at raglan edge only on next 2 rows. 3 sts. S1 1, K2 tog, psso, fasten off.

2nd size only

Dec one st at raglan edge only on next 4 rows. 4 sts. K2 tog tbl, K2 tog, pass first st over 2nd, fasten off.

3rd size only

Dec one st at raglan and neck edge on next row, then at raglan edge only on next 5 rows. 4 sts. Complete as given for 2nd size.

4th size only

Dec one st at raglan and neck edge on next row, then at raglan edge only on next 3 rows. Rep last 4 rows once more. 4 sts. Complete as given for 2nd size. ***

With RS of work facing, sl first 2 sts on to holder and leave for centre neck, rejoin yarn to rem sts, K2, patt to end. Work 3 rows without shaping then dec one st at neck edge on next row. Rep last 4 rows 3 times more, ending at side edge.

18th row Cast off 4 sts, patt to end.

Complete as given for left front from *** to *** reversing all shaping.

Sleeves

Using No. 3¼mm (10) needles cast on 58[62:66:70] sts. Work 19 rows rib as given for back, beg and ending with 2nd [1st:2nd:1st] row.

Next row (inc row) K2[4:6:8] sts, P2, PfB, P3, K2, P2, PfB, P4, PfB, P2, K2, (P2, PfB) 4 times, P2, K2, P2, PfB, P4, PfB, P2, K2, P2, PfB, P3, K2[4:6:8]. 68[72:76:80] sts.

Change to No. 4mm (8) needles. Commence patt.

1st row (RS) (K1 tbl, P1) 1[2:3:4] times, K7, P2, K12, P2, (Tr, TL) 3 times, P2, K12, P2, K7, (P1, K1 tbl) 1[2:3:4] times.

Cont in patt as now set with 2[4:6:8] sts in rice st at each end, 18 sts in honeycomb patt in centre, claw patt worked on groups of 7 sts and cable patt worked on groups of 12 sts. Cont in patt, inc one st at each end of 7th and every foll 8th [8th:7th:7th] row until there are 94 [100:106:112] sts, working extra sts into rice st. Cont without shaping until sleeve measures 48.5 [48.5:49.5:49.5]cm (*19[19:19½:19½]in*) from beg, ending with a WS row.

Shape raglan

Work as given for back from ** to **. Cast off rem 16[18:20:22] sts.

Back neckband

Using No. 3¼mm (10) needles and with RS of work facing, K up 42[42:46:46] sts across back neck. Beg with a 2nd row work 7 rows rib as given for back. Cast off in rib.

Front neckband

Join raglan edge of front to one raglan edge of each sleeve. Using No. 3¼mm (10) needles and with RS of work facing, K up 14[16:18:20] sts across left sleeve top, 78[80:82:84] sts down left front neck, K2 sts from holder, K up 78[80:82:84] sts up right front neck and 14[16:18:20] across right sleeve top. Work 2nd rib row as given for back.

Next row Rib 91[95:99:103] sts, K2 tog, K2 tog tbl, rib 91[95:99:103] sts.

Next row Rib 90[94:98:102] sts, P2 tog tbl, P2 tog, rib 90[94:98:102] sts.

Work six more rows rib, dec 2 sts in centre of each row. Cast off in rib, still dec in centre.

To make up

Do not press. Join back raglan seams and neckband edges. Join side and sleeve seams. Press seams lightly under a dry cloth with a cool iron.

His and hers jerseys

Sizes

To fit 86·5/89[92.5/95:99/101.5:105.5/108]cm (*34/35[36½/37½:39/40:41½/42½]in*) bust/chest
Length to shoulder, 68.5[70:72.5:73.5]cm (*27[27½:28½:29]in*)
Long sleeve seam, 47[47.5:49.5:50]cm (*18½[18¾:*

$19\frac{1}{2}:19\frac{3}{4}]in$), with cuff turned back

Short sleeve seam, 18[18.5:20.5:21]cm ($7[7\frac{1}{4}:8:8\frac{3}{4}:in$), with cuff turned back

The figures in brackets [ ] refer to the 92.5/95 ($36\frac{1}{2}/37\frac{1}{2}$), 99/101.5 (*39/40*) and 105.5/108cm ($41\frac{1}{2}/42\frac{1}{2}in$) sizes respectively

Tension
20 sts and 24 rows to 10cm (*3.9in*) over rice st worked on No. 4mm (*8*) needles

Materials
Blarney Bainin Wool
Long sleeved version 20[21:23:24] ×50grm balls
Short sleeved version 17[18:20:21] × 50 grm balls
One pair No. 4mm (*8*) needles
One pair No. $3\frac{3}{4}$mm (*9*) needles
One pair No. $3\frac{1}{4}$mm (*10*) needles
Two cable needles

Back
Using No. $3\frac{1}{4}$mm (*10*) needles cast on 106[110:114:118] sts.
1st row K2[P2:K2:P2], *P2, K2[K2, P2:P2, K2:K2, P2], rep from * to end.
2nd row P2[K2:P2:K2], *K2, P2[P2, K2:K2, P2:P2, K2], rep from * to end.
Rep these 2 rows 3[3:5:5] times more, then 1st row again.
Next row (inc row) (K2[3:4:5], K into front and back of next st — called Kfb—) twice, K2, *(P2, K2) 3 times, P2, P into front and back of next st — called Pfb —, P4, Pfb, P2, (K2, P2) 3 times, *, K2, (P2, Pfb) 6 times, K2, rep from * to * once more, (K2[3:4:5], Kfb) twice, K2. 120[124:128:132] sts.
Change to No. 4mm (*8*) needles. Commence patt.
1st row (RS) (K1 tbl, P1) 5[6:7:8] times, *(K2, P2) 3 times, K12, (P2, K2) 3 times, *, P2, (sl next 2 sts on to cable needle and hold at back of work, K1, then K2 from cable needle — called TR —, sl next st on to cable needle and hold at front of work, K2, then K1 from cable needle — called TL—) 4 times, P2, rep from * to * once more, (P1, K1 tbl) 5[6:7:8] times.
2nd and every alt row K10[12:14:16], *(P2, K2) 3 times, P12, (K2, P2) 3 times, *, K2, P24, K2, rep from * to * once more, K10[12:14:16].
3rd row (K1 tbl, P1) 5[6:7:8] times, *(K2, P2) 3 times, K12, (P2, K2) 3 times, *, P2, (TL, TR) 4 times, P2, rep from * to * once more, (Pl, K1 tbl) 5[6:7:8] times.
5th row (K1 tbl, P1) 5[6:7:8] times, * sl next 2 sts on to first cable needle and hold at front of work, sl next 2 sts on to second cable needle and hold at back of work, K2, P2 from cable needle at

back of work then K2 from cable needle at front of work — called Cr6l —, P2, K2, P2, sl next 3 sts on to cable needle and hold at back of work, K3 then K3 from cable needle — called C6b —, sl next 3 sts on to cable needle and hold at front of work, K3 then K3 from cable needle — called C6f —, P2, Cr6l, P2, K2, *, P2, (TR, TL) 4 times, P2, rep from * to * once more, (P1, K1 tbl) 5[6:7:8] times.
7th row As 3rd.
9th row As 1st.
11th row (K1 tbl, P1) 5[6:7:8] times, *K2, P2, sl next 4 sts on to cable needle and hold at back of work, K2, pass the 2 P sts from other end of cable needle back on to left hand needle, bring cable needle to front, P2 from left hand needle then K2 from cable needle — called Cr6r —, P2, C6b, C6f, P2, K2, P2, Cr6r, *, P2, (TL, TR) 4 times, P2, rep from * to * once more, (P1, K1 tbl) 5[6:7:8] times.
13th row As 1st.
15th row As 3rd.
17th row (K1 tbl, P1) 5[6:7:8] times, *Cr6l, P2, K2, P2, C6f, C6b, P2, Cr6l, P2, K2, *, P2, (TR, TL) 4 times, P2, rep from * to * once more, (P1, K1 tbl) 5[6:7:8] times.
19th row As 3rd.
21st Row As 1st.
23rd row (K1 tbl, P1) 5[6:7:8] times, *K2, P2, Cr6r, P2, C6f, C6b, P2, K2, P2, Cr6r, *, P2, (TL, TR) 4 times, P2, rep from * to * once more, (P1, K1 tbl) 5[6:7:8] times.
24th row As 2nd.
These 24 rows form patt and are rep throughout.
1st size only
Cont in patt dec one st at each end of 1st, 13th and 21st row of 2nd patt and 5th row of 3rd patt,

then inc one st at each end of row when work measures 33cm (*13in*) and 40·5cm (*16in*) from beg. 116 sts.

2nd size only
Cont in patt, dec one st at each end of 1st and 13th rows of 2nd patt and 1st row of 3rd patt, then inc one 1 st at each end of row when work measures 33cm (*13in*) and 40.5cm (*16in*) from beg. 122 sts.

4th size only
Cont in patt, inc one st at each end of row when work measures 23.5cm (*10in*) from beg. 134 sts.

All sizes
Cont without shaping until work measures 49.5[50:49.5:50]cm ($19\frac{1}{2}$[$19\frac{3}{4}$:$19\frac{1}{2}$:$19\frac{3}{4}$]*in*) from beg, ending with a WS row.

Shape armholes
Keeping patt correct, bind off 7 sts at beg of next 2 rows and 7[8:5:6] sts at beg of next 2 rows. 88[92:104:108] sts. Cont without shaping until armholes measure 19[19.5:23:23·5]cm ($7\frac{1}{2}$[$7\frac{3}{4}$:9:$9\frac{1}{4}$]*in*) from beg, ending with a WS row.

Shape shoulders
Cast off at beg of next and every row 8 sts 4[4:6:6] times and 12[14:8:10] sts twice. 32[32:40:40] sts.

Neckband
Change to No. $3\frac{3}{4}$mm (*9*) needles.
Next row (K2, P2) 1[1:2:2] times, (K2, K2 tog) 6 times, (P2, K2) 1[1:2:2] times. 26 [26:34:34] sts. Work 5 rows K2, P2 rib. Cast off loosely in rib.

Front
Work as given for back until front measures 6·5[5.5:4:3]cm ($2\frac{1}{2}$[$2\frac{1}{4}$:$1\frac{1}{2}$:$1\frac{1}{4}$]*in*) less than back to armholes, ending with a WS row.

Divide for neck
Next row Patt 55[58:61:64], K2, turn and leave rem sts on holder. 57[60:63:66] sts.
Dec one st at neck edge on every foll 3rd row 4[4:2:2] times in all. Work one more row, ending at side edge.

Shape armhole
Next row Cast off 7 sts, patt to end.
Next row Work 2 tog, patt to end.
Next row Cast off 7[8:5:6] sts, patt to end.
Keeping armhole edge straight, cont dec one st at neck edge on every 3rd row as before until 32[34: 32:34] sts rem.

1st and 2nd sizes only
Dec one st at neck edge on every foll 4th row 4 times in all. 28[30] sts.

All sizes
Cont without shaping until work measures same as back to shoulder, ending at armhole edge.

Shape shoulder
Cast off at beg of next and foll alt rows 8 sts

2[2:3:3] times and 12[14:8:10] sts once.
With RS of work facing, sl first 2 sts on to holder and leave for centre neck, rejoin yarn to rem sts, K2, patt to end.
Complete to match first side, reversing shaping.

Neckband
Using No. $3\frac{3}{4}$mm (*9*) needles and with RS of front facing, K up 68[68:76:76] sts down left front neck, K across 2 centre front sts from holder and K up 68[68:76:76] sts up right front neck. 138[138:154:154] sts. Work 2nd row as given for back.
Next row Rib 67[67:75:75], K2 tog, K2 tog tbl, rib to end.
Next row Rib 66[66:74:74], P2 tog tbl, P2 tog, rib to end.
Work 2 more rows rib, dec one st at either side of centre. Cast off in rib, dec as before.

Long sleeves
Using No. $3\frac{3}{4}$mm (*9*) needles cast on 46[50:54:58] sts. Beg with 1st[2nd:1st:2nd] rib row work 6.5[6.5:7.5:7.5]cm ($2\frac{1}{2}$[$2\frac{1}{2}$:3:3]*in*) rib as given for back. Change to No. $3\frac{1}{4}$mm (*10*) needles. Work a further 6.5[6.5:7.5:7.5]cm ($2\frac{1}{2}$[$2\frac{1}{2}$:3:3]*in*) rib, ending with a 2nd row.
Next row (inc row) K2[4:6:8] sts, (P2, K2) 3 times, (P2, Pfb) 6 times, (K2, P2) 3 times, K2[4:6:8]. 52[56:60:64] sts.
Change to No. 4mm (*8*) needles. Commence patt.
1st row (K1 tbl, P1) 1[2:3:4] times, (K2, P2) 3 times, (TR, TL) 4 times, (P2, K2) 3 times, (P1, K1 tbl) 1[2:3:4] times.
Cont in patt as set, work 3 rows without shaping. Inc one st at each end of next and every foll 6th row until there are 78[80:90:92] sts, working extra sts into rice st. Cont without shaping until work measures 53.5[54:57:57.5]cm (*21*[$21\frac{1}{4}$:$22\frac{1}{2}$:$22\frac{3}{4}$]*in*) from beg. Place markers of contrast yarn at each end of last row, then work a further 18[19:16:17] rows.

Shape top
Cast off at beg of next and every row 4 sts 8[8:10: 10] times and 5[6:6:7] sts 4 times. Cast off rem 26[24:26:24] sts.

Short sleeves
Using No. $3\frac{3}{4}$mm (*9*) needles cast on 62[66:70:74] sts. Work 6.5cm ($2\frac{1}{2}$*in*) rib as given for long sleeves. Change to No. $3\frac{1}{4}$mm (*10*) needles. Work a further 6.5cm ($2\frac{1}{2}$*in*) rib, ending with a 2nd row.
Next row (inc row) K10[12:14:16], (P2, K2) 3 times, (P2, Pfb) 6 times, (K2, P2) 3 times, K10[12:14:16]. 68[72:76:80] sts.
Change to No. 4mm (*8*) needles. Commence patt.
1st row (K1 tbl, P1) 5[6:7:8] times, (K2, P2)

3 times, (TR, TL) 4 times, (P2, K2) 3 times, (P1, K1 tbl) 5[6:7:8] times.

Cont in patt as set, inc one st at each end of next and every foll 4th row until there are 78[80:90:92] sts, working extra sts into rice st. Cont without shaping until work measures 24[24.5:26·5:27]cm ($9\frac{1}{2}$[$9\frac{3}{4}$:$10\frac{1}{2}$:$10\frac{3}{4}$]in) from beg. Place markers of contrast yarn at each end of last row, then work a further 18[19:16:17] rows.

Shape top

Work as given for long sleeves.

To make up

Press each piece lightly under a damp cloth with a warm iron. Join shoulder and neckband seams. Set in sleeves, sewing row ends of sleeves above markers to cast off edge at beg of armhole shaping. Join side and sleeve seams, reversing seam on cuffs. Press seams.

Aran set

Sizes

Jersey to fit 86.5/91.5[96.5/101.5]cm (34/36[38/40] in) bust

Length to shoulder, 67.5[69]cm ($26\frac{1}{2}$[$27\frac{1}{4}$]in)

Sleeve seam, 47[48.5]cm ($18\frac{1}{2}$[19]in)

Scarf length, 170.5cm (67in)

Hat to fit an average adult head

Mitts to fit an average adult hand

The figures in brackets[] refer to the 96.5/101.5cm (38/40in) bust size only

Tension

13 sts and 11 rows to 7.5cm (3in) over bramble patt worked on No. 6½mm (3) needles

Materials

Jersey 17[19]×50grm balls Claude by 3 Suisse

Scarf 7 balls of same

Hat 3 balls of same

Mitts 3 balls of same

One pair No. 6½mm (3) needles

One pair No. 6mm (4) needles

One pair No. 5mm (6) needles

Cable needle

One No. 5.00 (ISR) crochet hook

Jersey front

Using No. 5mm (6) needles cast on 76[86] sts. Work 7.5cm (3in) K1, P1 rib, inc one st at centre of last row on first size only. 77[86] sts. Change to No. 6½mm (3) needles. Commence patt.

1st row (RS) P4[5], *K6, P3[4], rep from * to last st, P1.

2nd row K4[5], *P6, K3[4], rep from * to last st, K1.

Rep last 2 rows once more.

5th row P4[5], *sl next 3 sts on to cable needle and leave at back of work, K3, then K3 sts from cable needle — called C6B —, P3[4], rep from * to last st, P1.

6th row As 2nd.

These 6 rows form cable patt. Cont in cable patt until 21 rows in all have been worked.

22nd row Patt to end, inc one st at centre of row on first size only. 78[86] sts.

Commence bramble patt.

23rd row P to end.

24th row K1, *(K1, P1, K1) into next st, P3 tog, rep from * to last st, K1.

25th row P to end.

26th row K1, *P3 tog, (K1, P1, K1) into next st, rep from * to last st, K1.

Rep 23rd — 26th rows once more, then 23rd — 25th rows again.

34th row Patt to end, but for first size only, at approx centre of row, work (K1, P1) into one st instead of (K1, P1, K1). 77[86] sts.

Rep last 34 rows once more. 4 complete patt panels. Cont throughout in cable patt.

Shape armholes

Next row Cast off 5 sts, K until there are 5 sts on right hand needle, *P3, K6, rep from * to last 4 sts, P4.

Next row Cast off 5 sts, patt as set to end.

Keeping patt correct, cast off 4[6] sts at beg of next 2 rows. 59[64] sts. Cont without shaping in cable patt until armholes measure 14[16]cm ($5\frac{1}{2}$[$6\frac{1}{4}$]in) from beg, ending with a WS row. **.

Shape neck

Next row Patt 25[27] sts, turn and leave rem sts on holder.

Complete this side first. Cast off at beg (neck edge) of next and foll alt rows 3 sts once, 2 sts twice and one st twice, ending at armhole edge.

Shape shoulder

Cast off at beg of next and foll alt rows 6 sts twice and 4[6] sts once.

With RS of work facing, rejoin yarn to rem sts, cast off first 9[10] sts for centre neck, patt to end. Work one row. Complete as given for first side, reversing shaping.

Back

Work as given for front to **. Patt 8 more rows.

Shape neck and shoulders

Next row Patt 22[24] sts, turn and leave rem sts on holder.

Complete this side first. Cast off at beg of next and every row (2 sts once and 6 sts once) twice,

2 sts once and 4[6] sts once.
With RS of work facing, rejoin yarn to rem sts,
cast off first 15[16] sts for centre back neck,
patt to end. Work one row. Complete as given for
first side, reversing shaping.

Sleeves
Using No. 5mm (*6*) needles cast on 40[46] sts.

Work 6.5[7.5]cm (2½[*3*]*in*) K1, P1 rib.
Next row (inc row) Rib 8[6], *inc in next st, rib
3[4], rep from * to end. 48[54] sts.
Change to No. 6½mm (*3*) needles. Commence
cable patt.
1st row (RS) P3[4], *K6, P3[4], rep from * to end.
Cont working in cables in positions as now set,
inc one st at each end of 4th, 8th, 12th, 16th and

20th rows of cable patt panel, keeping extra sts at sides in rev st st. 58[64] sts. Patt 2 more rows. Commence bramble patt as given for front, noting that for 2nd size only WS rows will begin and end with K2 instead of K1. Patt 11 rows.
Next row Inc in first st, K0[1], *P3 tog, (K1, P1, K1) into next st, rep from * to last 1[2] sts, K0 [1], inc in last st. 60[66] sts.
Change to cable patt.
Next row K6, *P3[4], K6, rep from * to end.
Cont in patt as now set, inc one st at each end of 4th, 8th and 12th rows of patt panel and working cable over inc sts at each side. Cont on 66[72] sts without shaping until 22 rows of cable patt have been completed. Change to bramble patt as previously given for sleeves, but working 12 rows without shaping. Change to cable patt with cables arranged as at end of last cable patt panel. Cont without shaping until side edges of this panel fit along cast off edge at back and front underarms, ending with a WS row.

Shape top
Cast off 5 sts at beg of next 2 rows and 4[5] sts at beg of foll 2 rows. Rep last 4 rows twice more. Cast off rem 12 sts.

Neckband
Join right shoulder seam. Using No. 5mm (6) needles and with RS of work facing, K up 46[50] sts around front neck edge and 36[40] sts round back neck edge. 82[90] sts. Work 5 rows K1, P1 rib. Cast off loosely in rib.

To make up
Join left shoulder and neckband seams. Set in sleeves, sew top all around armhole and side edge of cable patt to cast off sts at underarm. Join side and sleeve seams. Press seams under a damp cloth with a warm iron.

Scarf
Using No. 6mm (4) needles cast on 40 sts.
Commence bramble patt.
1st row (RS) K2, P36, K2.
2nd row K2, *(K1, P1, K1) into next st, P3 tog, rep from * to last 2 sts, K2.
Cont in bramble patt as now set, keeping 2 sts at each side in g st until 11 rows have been completed.
Next row K2, (P3 tog, K1, P1, K1 into next st) 4 times, P3 tog, K1, P1 into next st, (P3 tog, K1, P1, K1 into next st) 4 times, K2. 39 sts.
**Change to No. 6½mm (3) needles. Commence cable patt.
Next row K2, P1, (K6, P3) 3 times, K6, P1, K2.
Cont in cable patt, with g st borders as now set until 22 rows have been completed, inc one st in

centre of last row 40 sts. Change to No. 6mm (4) needles. Work 12 more rows bramble patt. **.
Rep from ** to ** 7 times more. Cast off using No. 6mm (4) needles.

To make up
Lightly press each cable panel on WS under a damp cloth with a warm iron, stretching them to width of bramble patt panels.

Fringe
Cut lengths of yarn 25.5cm (10in) long, and, using 3 strands tog, make 14 knots along each short end.

Hat
Using No. 6½mm (3) needles cast on 86 sts. Work in bramble patt as given for front of jersey, but rep the 4 patt rows 4 times in all. Change to No. 6mm (4) needles. Work the 4 patt rows again.
Next row K2,K2 tog, *P6, K3, rep from * to last 10 sts, P6, K2 tog, K2. 84 sts.
Change to cable patt, beg with a RS row so reversing brim.
Next row P3, *K6, P3, rep from * to end.
Cont in cable patt as now set until 1st patt is completed. Change to No. 6½mm (3) needles. Cont in patt until 3rd patt is completed.

Shape top
Next row P2 tog, P1, *K6, P1, P2 tog, rep from * to end.
Work 3 rows patt, keeping 2 sts in each rev st st panel.
Next row: P2, *sl next 3 sts on to cable needle

and leave at back of work, K3 then K2 tog, K1 from cable needle, P2, rep from * to end.
Next row K2, *P5, K2, rep from * to end.
Next row *P1, K2 tog, K4, rep from * to last 2 sts, P2 tog.
Next row K1, *P5, K1, rep from * to end.
Next row *K2 tog, K1, rep from * to last 4 sts, (K2 tog) twice.
Next row *P1, P2 tog, P1, rep from * to end.
Next row *Sl 1, K2 tog, psso, rep from * to end.
Break off yarn leaving a long end, thread through rem sts, draw up and fasten off securely.

To make up
Join back seam, reversing it for brim on bramble patt section. Press seam. Turn first 16 rows of bramble patt to RS to form brim. Make a pom-pon and sew to top.

Mitts left hand
Using No. 6mm (4) needles cast on 38 sts. Change to No. 6½mm (3) needles. Work 9 rows bramble patt as given for front of jersey.
Next row K1, (K1, P1, K1 into next st, P3 tog) 4 times, K1, P1, K1 into next st, P2 tog, P1, (K1, P1, K1 into next st, P3 tog) 4 times, K1. 39 sts.
Cont in cable patt, setting patt as given for hat, until 2nd row of 1st patt has been completed.
Shape thumb
Next row Patt 18, pick up loop lying between needles and P tbl — called M1 —, P1, M1, P2, patt 18.
Next row Patt 18, K5, patt 18.
Next row (P3, C6B) twice, M1, P3, M1, P2, (C6B, P3) twice.
Next row (K3, P6) twice, K7, (P6, K3) twice.
Next row Patt 18, M1, P5, M1, P2, patt 18.
Next row (K3, P6) twice, K9, (P6, K3) twice.
Next row Patt 18, M1, P7, M1, P2, patt 18.
Next row Patt 18, K11, patt 18.
Next row (P3, C6B) twice and leave these 18 sts on holder for palm, P9, cast on one st, turn and leave rem 20 sts on holder for back of hand.
Work 9 rows reversed st st on these 10 thumb sts.
Next row (P2 tog) 5 times.
Break off yarn leaving a long end, thread through rem sts, draw up and fasten off securely.
With RS of work facing, rejoin yarn to base of thumb, K one st from base, patt across 20 sts of back of hand.
Next row (K3, P6) twice, K3, cont in patt across 18 sts on palm on holder. 39 sts.
Cont in patt until 5th patt from beg has been completed, then work 3 rows of next patt.
Next row K2 tog, K1, *P6, K1, K2 tog, rep from * to end.

Next row P2, *(K2 tog) 3 times, P2, rep from * to end. 22 sts.
Break off yarn, sl first 11 sts on to other needle, fold work in half with RS inside and two points tog, then using spare needle cast off working a st from each needle tog all across. Fasten off.

Right mitt
Work as given for left hand until thumb shaping is reached.
Shape thumb
Next row Patt 18, P2, M1, P1, M1, patt 18.
Cont working incs as set until there are 47 sts.
Next row Patt 18, K11, patt 18.
Next row (P3, C6B) twice, P2 and leave these 20 sts on holder for back of hand, P9, turn and leave rem 18 sts on holder for palm.
Next row K9, turn and cast on one st.
Complete thumb as given for left hand.
With RS of work facing, rejoin yarn to base of thumb, K one st from base of thumb, patt across 18 sts of palm.
Next row Patt 19, cont in patt across 20 sts of back of hand.
Complete as given for left hand.

To make up
Join thumb and side seams. Press seams. Using No. 5.00 (ISR) hook and yarn double, make a crochet chain approx 45.5cm (18in) long. Thread through last row of bramble patt, beg and ending at centre back of hand. Trim ends of chain with small pom-pon.

Aran bag and belt

Size
Belt to fit 61/63.5[66/70]cm (24/25[26/27]in) waist
Bag 12.5cm (5½in) deep × 26.5cm (10½in) long
The figures in brackets [] refer to the 66/70cm (26/27in) waist size

Tension
20 sts and 24 rows to 10cm (3.9in) over patt worked on No. 4½mm (7) needles

Materials
Belt 1 × 50grm ball Sirdar Pullman
Bag 2 balls of same
One pair No. 4½mm (7) needles

One cable needle
One belt fastener

Belt

Using No. 4½mm (7) needles cast on 12 sts.
Commence patt.
1st row K1, P3, K4, P3, K1.
2nd row K4, P4, K4.
Rep these 2 rows twice more, then first row again.
8th row K4, P1, sl 2 P-wise keeping yarn at front of work, P1, K4.
9th row K1, P1, sl next 3 sts on to cable needle and hold at back of work, K1, then P1, K1, P1 from cable needle — called C4B —, sl next st on to cable needle and hold at front of work, K1, P1, K1 then K1 from cable needle — called C4F —, P1, K1.
10th row K2, (P1, K1) 3 times, P2, K2.
11th row (K1, P1) 4 times, K2, P1, K1.
Rep 10th and 11th rows twice more.
16th row K2, sl 1 P-wise holding yarn at front of work, ybk, (K1, P1) 3 times, sl 1 P-wise holding yarn at front of work, ybk, K2.
17th row K1, P1, sl next st on to cable needle and hold at front of work, P2, K1, K1 from cable needle — called C4FP —, sl next 3 sts on to cable needle and hold at back of work, K1, then K1, P2 from cable needle — called C4BP —, P1, K1.
18th row As 2nd.
These 18 rows form patt and are rep throughout.
Cont in patt until 7[8] complete patts have been worked, then rep 1st and 2nd rows 3 times more.
Cast off in patt.

To make up

Press lightly under a damp cloth with a warm iron. Sew fastener to cast on and cast off edges.

Bag

Using No. 4½mm (7) needles cast on 54 sts.
Commence patt.
1st row K1, *P4, K4, rep from * to last 5 sts, P4, K1.
2nd row K1, *K4, P4, rep from * to last 5 sts, K5.
Rep 1st and 2nd rows once more, then 1st row again.
6th row K1, *K4, P1, sl 2 P-wise holding yarn at front of work, P1, rep from * to last 5 sts, K5.
7th row K1, P2, *C4B, C4F, rep from * to last 3 sts, P2, K1.
8th row K3, *(P1, K1) 3 times, P2, rep from * to last 3 sts, K3.
9th row K1, P2, *(K1, P1) 3 times, K2, rep from * to last 3 sts, P2, K1.
Rep 8th and 9th rows twice more.
14th row K3, sl 1 P-wise keeping yarn at front of work, ybk, *(K1, P1) 3 times, sl 2 P-wise keeping yarn at front of work, ybk, rep from * to last 10 sts, (K1, P1) 3 times, sl 1, ybk, K3.
15th row K1, P2, *C4FP, C4BP, rep from * to last 3 sts, P2, K1.
16th row As 2nd.
17th row As 1st.
18th row As 2nd.
Rep these 18 rows once more. Rep 1st and 2nd rows only until work measures 39.5cm (15½in) from beg, ending with a WS row. Cast off in patt.

To make up

Press as given for belt. Fold 12.5cm (5in) from cast off edge on to WS and oversew edges neatly. Press seams lightly.
This beautiful aran belt can be worn with trousers, skirts, or over a jersey dress. Team it with a clutch bag in matching aran stitches, for a co-ordinated accessory wardrobe. These designs can be made in an evening and will look stunning.

Fair Isle stitch library

Traditional Fair Isle patterns produce beautiful designs and fabrics, which are world-renowned for their subtle combinations. Ideally, they should be worked in the authentic, softly shaded yarn but they look just as effective when worked in bright, contrasting colours.

These patterns may be used to form an all-over fabric or as a border to highlight the welt and sleeves of a basic jersey or cardigan. When the pattern is small and is repeated as an all-over design, it is a fairly simple matter to work from a chart, where each colour in the pattern is shown as a separate symbol. Some knitters, however, experience difficulty in working from a chart when

the pattern is large and fairly complex, particularly, where shaping is required. In this event, it is preferable to work from a pattern which gives row-by-row instructions, where each separate colour is coded with a letter, such as A, B or C. To help you decide which method you wish to follow, the patterns here have been given with row by row instructions.

Fair Isle pattern No. 1
Cast on multiples of 12 stitches plus 6.
1st row *K3 A, 1 B, 5 A, 1 B, 2 A, rep from * to last 6 sts, 3 A, 1 B, 2 A.
2nd row *(P1 A, 1 B) twice, 2 A, rep from * to end.
3rd row *K1 A, 1 B, 3 A, 1 B, rep from * to end.
4th row As 2nd.
5th row *K1 B, 2 A, rep from * to end.
6th row *(P1 B, 1 A) twice, 2 B, rep from * to end.
7th row *K2 B, (1 A, 1 B) twice, rep from * to end.
Rep 6th and 7th rows once more.
10th row *P2 A, 1 B, rep from * to end.
11th row *K2 A, (1 B, 1 A) twice, rep from * to end.
12th row *P1 B, 3 A, 1 B, 1 A, rep from * to end.
13th row As 11th.
14th row *P2 A, 1 B, 5 A, 1 B, 3 A, rep from * to last 6 sts, 2 A, 1 B, 3 A.
15th row *K1 B, 5 A, rep from * to end.
16th row *P1 B, 3 A, 1 B, 1 A, rep from * to end.
17th row *K2 A, (1 B, 1 A) twice, rep from * to end.
18th row As 16th.
19th row *K1 B, 2 A, rep from * to end.
20th row *P1 A, 3 B, 1 A, 1 B, rep from * to end.
21st row *K1 B, 1 A, 3 B, 1 A, rep from * to end.

Rep 20th and 21st rows once more.
24th row *P2 A, 1 B, rep from * to end.
25th row *K1 A, 1 B, 3 A, 1 B, rep from * to end.
26th row *(P1 A, 1B) twice, 2 A, rep from * to end.
27th row As 25th.
28th row *P5 A, 1 B, rep from * to end.
These 28 rows form the pattern.

Fair Isle pattern No. 2
Cast on multiples of 18 stitches plus 1.
1st row *K1 B, 1 A, rep from * to last st, 1 B.
2nd row Using A, P to end.
3rd row Using A, K to end.
4th row *P1 C, 1 A, 1 C, 6 A, 1 C, 6 A, 1 C, 1 A, rep from * to last st, 1 C.
5th row *K2 C, 1 A, 1 C, 4 A, 3 C, 4 A, 1 C, 1 A, 1 C, rep from * to last st, 1 C.
6th row *P1 C, 3 A, 1 C, 2 A, 2 C, 1 A, 2 C, 2 A, 1 C, 3 A, rep from * to last st, 1 C.
7th row *K1 C, 4 A, 1 C, 1 A, 5 C, 1 A, 1 C, 4 A, rep from * to last st, 1 C.
8th row *P1 A, 1 C, 4 A, 3 C, 1 A, 3 C, 4 A, 1 C, rep from * to last st, 1 A.
9th row *K1 B, 3 A, 3 B, 2 A, 1 B, 2 A, 3 B, 3 A, rep from * to last st, 1 B.
10th row *P3 A, 4 B, (1 A, 1 B) twice, 1 A, 4 B, 2 A, rep from * to last st, 1 A.
11th row *K2 A, 2 B, (1 A, 1 B) 5 times, 1 A, 2 B, 1 A, rep from * to last st, 1 A.
Rep 10th to 1st rows. These 21 rows form border pattern, working 22nd row for all-over pattern.

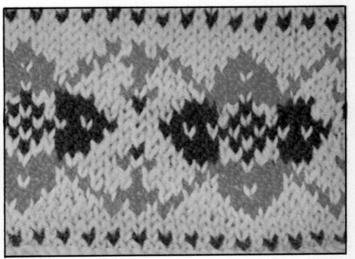

Fair Isle pattern No. 3
Cast on multiples of 18 stitches plus 1.
1st row *K1 B, 1 A, rep from * to last st, 1 B.
2nd row *P1 A, 1 B, rep from * to last st, 1 A.
3rd row Using A, K to end.
4th row Using A, P to end.
5th row As 3rd.

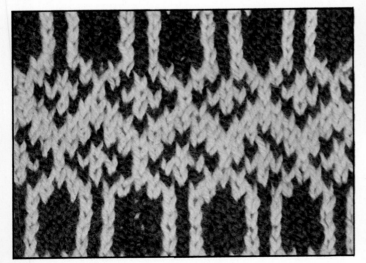

6th row *P3 A, 1 C, 5 A, 1 C, 5 A, 1 C, 2 A, rep from * to last st, 1 A.
7th row *K2 A, 2 C, 4 A, 3 C, 4 A, 2 C, 1 A, rep from * to last st, 1 A.
8th row *P1 A, 3 C, 5 A, 1 C, 5 A, 3 C, rep from * to last st, 1 A.
9th row *K1 D, 2 C, 2 D, 3 C, 3 D, 3 C, 2 D, 2 C, rep from * to last st, 1 D.
10th row *P1 D, 1 C, 2 D, 3 C, 5 D, 3 C, 2 D, 1 C, rep from * to last st, 1 D.
11th row *K1 B, 2 E, 3 B, 3 E, 1 B, 3 E, 3 B, 2 E, rep from * to last st, 1 B.
12th row *P1 F, 2 B, 5 F, 3 B, 5 F, 2 B, rep from * to last st, 1 F.
Rep 11th to 3rd rows.
22nd row *P1 B, 1 A, rep from * to last st, 1 B.
23rd row *K1 A, 1 B, rep from * to last st, 1 A.
These 23 rows form border pattern, repeating 22 rows only for all-over pattern.

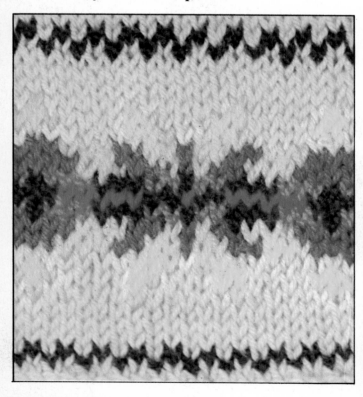

Fair Isle pattern No. 4
Cast on multiples of 28 stitches plus 1.
1st row *K2 B, 1 A, 1 B, rep from * to last st, 1 B.
2nd row *P1 B, 3 A, rep from * to last st, 1 B.
3rd row Using A, K to end.
4th row *P1 A, 2 C, 2 A, 2 C, 2 A, 2 C, 3 A, 1 C, 3 A, 2 C, 2 A, 2 C, 2 A, 2 C, rep from * to last st, 1 A.
5th row *K1 A, 1 C, (2 A, 2 C) twice, 3 A, 1 C, 1 A, 1 C, 3 A, (2 C, 2 A) twice, 1 C, rep from * to last st, 1 A.

6th row *P1 A, 1 C, 1 A, 2 C, 2 A, 2 C, 3 A, (1 C, 1 A) twice, 1 C, 3 A, 2 C, 2 A, 2 C, 1 A, 1 C, rep from * to last st, 1 A.
7th row *K1 A, 3 C, 2 A, 2 C, 3 A, 1 C, 1 A, 3 C, 1 A, 1 C, 3 A, 2 C, 2 A, 3 C, rep from * to last st, 1 A.
8th row *P1 A, 2 C, 2 A, 2 C, 3 A, 1 C, 2 A, 3 C, 2 A, 1 C, 3 A, 2 C, 2 A, 2 C, rep from * to last st, 1 A.
9th row *K1 A, 1 D, 2 A, 2 D, 3 A, 3 D, 2 A, 1 D, 2 A, 3 D, 3 A, 2 D, 2 A, 1 D, rep from * to last st, 1 A.
10th row *P1 A, 1 D, 1 A, 2 D, 3 A, 1 D, 2 A, 2 D, 1 A, 1 D, 1 A, 2 D, 2 A, 1 D, 3 A, 2 D, 1 A, 1 D, rep from * to last st, 1 A.
11th row *K1 A, 3 D, 3 A, 2 D, 3 A, 5 D, 3 A, 2 D, 3 A, 3 D, rep from * to last st, 1 A.
12th row *P1 A, 2 D, 3 A, 1 D, 1 A, 2 D, 3 A, 3 D, 3 A, 2 D, 1 A, 1 D, 3 A, 2 D, rep from * to last st, 1 A.
13th row *K1 A, 1 D, 3 A, 1 D, 3 A, 2 D, 3 A, 1 D, 3 A, 2 D, 3 A, 1 D, 3 A, 1 D, rep from * to last st, 1 A.
14th row *P1 A, 1 D, 2 A, 1 D, 1 A, 2 D, 2 A, 2 D, (1A, 1D) twice, 1 A, 2 D, 2 A, 2 D, 1 A, 1 D, 2 A, 1 D, rep from * to last st, 1 A.
15th row *K1 A, (1 B, 1 A) twice, 8 B, 1 A, 1 B, 1 A, 8 B, (1 A, 1 B) twice, rep from * to last st, 1 A.
Rep from 14th to 1st rows. These 29 rows form border pattern, working 30th row for all-over pattern.

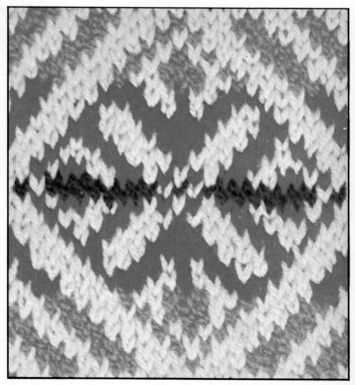

Fair Isle design collection

Fair Isle jersey

Sizes
To fit 81.5[86.5:91.5:96.5]cm (*32[34:36:38]in*) bust
Length to shoulder, 56[57:58:59]cm (*22[22½:22¾: 23¼]in*)
Sleeve seam, 43[44:45:46]cm (*17[17¼:17¾:18]in*)
The figures in brackets [] refer to the 86.5 (*34*), 91.5 (*36*) and 96.5cm (*38in*) sizes respectively

Tension
28 sts and 36 rows to 10cm (*3.9in*) over st st worked on No. 3¼mm (*10*) needles

Materials
8[9:9:10] × 25grm balls Templeton's H. & O. Shetland Fleece in main shade, A
1 ball in each of 7 contrast colours, B, C, D, E, F, G and H
One pair No. 3¼mm (*10*) needles
One pair No. 2¾mm (*12*) needles
One No. 3.00 (ISR) crochet hook
3 buttons

Back
Using No. 2¾mm (*12*) needles and A, cast on 113[113:127:127] sts.
1st row K1, *P1, K1, rep from * to end.
2nd row P1, *K1, P1, rep from * to end.
Rep these 2 rows until work measures 7cm (*2¾in*) from beg, ending with a 2nd row. Change to No. 3¼mm (*10*) needles. Beg with a K row, work 2 rows st st. Cont in st st, patt 19 rows from chart, using colours as required. Cont in A only until work measures 39cm (*15¼in*) from beg, ending with a P row.
Shape armholes
Cast off 5[2:5:2] sts at beg of next 2 rows and 2[2:3:3] sts at beg of foll 2 rows. 99[105:111:117] sts.
Next row K1, sl 1, K1, psso, K to last 3 sts, K2 tog, K1.

33

Chart for sleeves and neckband

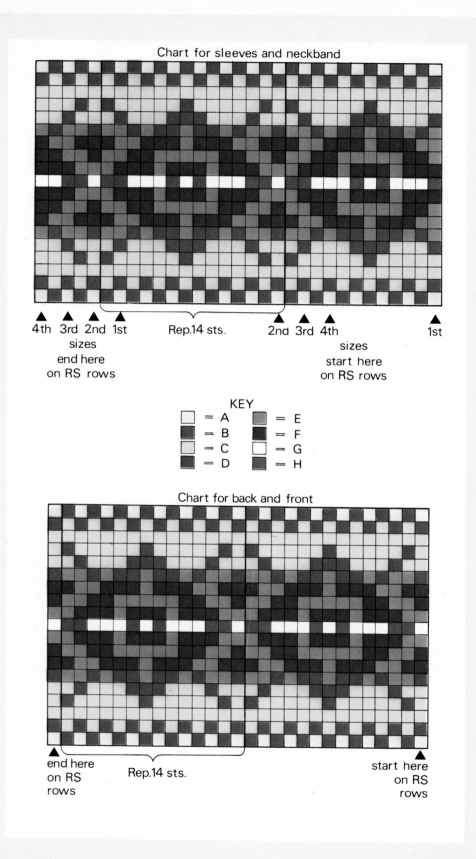

4th 3rd 2nd 1st

sizes
end here
on RS rows

Rep.14 sts.

2nd 3rd 4th

sizes
start here
on RS rows

1st

KEY

☐ = A   ◩ = E
◪ = B   ■ = F
▨ = C   ☐ = G
◧ = D   ▤ = H

Chart for back and front

end here
on RS
rows

Rep.14 sts.

start here
on RS
rows

Next row P to end.
Rep last 2 rows 3[4:5:6] times more. 91[95:99:103] sts. Cont without shaping until armholes measure 13[14:15:16]cm (5[5½:6:6¼]in) from beg, ending with a P row.
Shape neck and shoulders
Next row K36[37:38:39] sts, turn and leave rem sts on holder.
Complete this side first. Cast off 2 sts at beg of next and foll 5 alt rows, ending at armhole edge. 24[25:26:27] sts.
Next row Cast off 8 sts, K to last 2 sts, K2 tog.
Next row P to end.
Rep last 2 rows once more. Cast off 6[7:8:9] sts.
With RS of work facing, sl first 19[21:23:25] sts on holder and leave for centre back neck, rejoin yarn to next st and K to end. Complete to match first side, reversing shaping.

Front
Using No. 2¾mm (*12*) needles and A, cast on 113[127:127:141] sts. Work as given for back to underarm, ending with a P row.
Shape armholes
Cast off 5[9:5:9] sts at beg of next 2 rows and 2[2:3:3] sts at beg of foll 2 rows. 99[105:111:117] sts. Dec one st as given for back at each end of next and foll 3[4:5:6] alt rows. 91[95:99:103] sts.
Cont without shaping until armhole measures 8[9:10:11]cm (3¼[3½:4:4¼]in) from beg, ending with a P row.
Shape neck
Next row K38[39:40:41] sts, turn and leave rem sts on holder.
Complete this side first. Cast off 2 sts at beg of next and foll 4 alt rows, ending at armhole edge.
Next row K to last 3 sts, sl 1, K1, psso, K1.
Next row P to end.
Rep last 2 rows 5 times more. 22[23:24:25] sts.
Cont without shaping until armhole measures same as back to shoulder, ending at armhole edge.
Shape shoulder
Cast off at beg of next and foll alt rows 8 sts twice and 6[7:8:9] sts once.
With RS of work facing, sl first 15[17:19:21] sts on holder and leave for centre front neck, rejoin yarn to next st and K to end. Complete to match first side, reversing shaping.

Sleeves
Using No. 2¾mm (*12*) needles and A, cast on 53[57:61:65] sts. Work 7cm (2¾in) rib as given for back, ending with a 2nd row. Change to No. 3¼mm (*10*) needles. Beg with a K row, work 2 rows st st. Cont in st st, patt 19 rows from chart. Cont in A only, P1 row. Inc one st at each end of next and every foll 6th row until there are

85[89:93:97] sts. Cont without shaping until sleeve measures 43[44:45:46]cm (17[17¼:17¾:18] in) from beg, ending with a P row. Mark this point with a coloured thread. Work 8 more rows.
Shape top
Next row K1, sl 1, K1, psso, K to last 3 sts, K2 tog, K1.
Next row P to end.
Rep last 2 rows 11[12:13:14] times more. 61[63:65:67] sts. Cast off 2 sts at beg of next 12 rows and 3 sts at beg of foll 10 rows. Cast off rem 7[9:11:13] sts.

Neckband
Join right shoulder seam. Using No. 3¼mm (*10*) needles, A and with RS of work facing, K up 34 sts down left front neck, K across centre front neck sts on holder, K up 33 sts up right front neck, 18 sts down right back neck, K across centre back neck sts on holder and K up 18 sts up left back neck. 137[141:145:149] sts. P1 row, then patt 19 rows from chart, dec 20 sts evenly across 17th row of patt. 117[121:125:129] sts. Change to No. 2¾mm (*12*) needles. P 1 row, then work 3cm (1¼in) rib as given for back. Cast off in rib.

To make up
Press under a damp cloth with a warm iron. Join left shoulder seam for 1cm (½in) from shoulder edge. Fold neckband in half to WS and sl st down. Set in sleeves, sewing last 8 row ends of sleeves to cast off sts at underarm, noting that on 2nd and 4th sizes the side seam will come to the back of sleeve seam. Join side and sleeve seams. Press seams. Using No. 3.00 (ISR) crochet hook and A, work a row of dc all round left shoulder opening, making 3 button loops on front edge. Sew on buttons to correspond.

Three in Fair Isle

Sizes
Scarf 167.5cm (*66in*) long × 21cm (*8¼in*) wide
Hat to fit average woman's head
Mitts to fit average woman's hands

Tension
28 sts and 36 rows to 10cm (*3.9in*) over st st worked on No. 3¼mm (*10*) needles

Materials

7 × 25grm balls Templeton's H. & O. Shetland
Fleece in main shade, A
2 balls each of contrast colours, B, C, D, E and F
1 ball each of contrast colours, G and H
One set of 4 No1 3¼mm (10) needles pointed at
both ends
One set of 4 No. 2¾mm (12) needles pointed
at both ends

Scarf

Using set of 4 No. 3¼mm (10) needles and A,
cast on 116 sts. K 3 rounds. Cont working in patt
from chart, rep 31 rounds, until work measures
164.5cm (64¾in) from beg, ending with 31st
round. Work first 2 rounds from chart once more.
K3 rounds in A. Cast off.

To make up

Press under a damp cloth with a warm iron.

Fringe

Using any colour, cut lengths of yarn each approx
45.5cm (18in) long. Taking 6 strands tog, knot
fringe along cast on and cast off edges.

Hat

Using set of 4 No. 3¼mm (10) needles and A,
cast on 144 sts. Cont in rounds of K1, P1 rib
until work measures 7cm (2¾in) from beg. Change
to set of 4 No. 2¾mm (12) needles. Cont in rib
until work measures 11cm (4¼in) from beg, inc
one st at end of last round. 145 sts. Change to
set of 4 No. 3¼mm (10) needles. K 4 rounds.
Work 33 rounds in patt from chart. Using A,
cont working in st st throughout. K 2 rounds,
dec one st at end of last round. 144 sts.

Shape top

Next round *K10, K2 tog, rep from * to end.
132 sts.
Next round K to end.
Next round *K9, K2 tog, rep from * to end.
120 sts.
Cont dec 12 sts in this way on every foll alt
round until 24 sts rem, ending with a K round.
Next round *K2 tog, rep from * to end. 12 sts.
Break off yarn, thread through rem sts, draw up
and fasten off.

To make up

Press as given for scarf. Fold brim in half to RS.

Mitts right hand

Using set of 4 No. 2¾mm (12) needles and A,
cast on 56 sts. Cont in rounds of K1, P1 rib until
work measures 8cm (3¼in) from beg, inc 8 sts

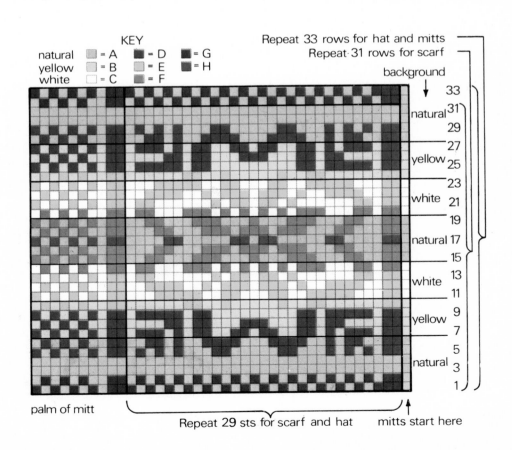

KEY

natural ■ = A ■ = D ■ = G
yellow ■ = B ■ = E ■ = H
white □ = C ■ = F

Repeat 33 rows for hat and mitts
Repeat 31 rows for scarf

background

palm of mitt

Repeat 29 sts for scarf and hat   mitts start here

evenly across last round. 64 sts. K 6 rounds.
Commence patt.
1st round K1 A, 3 B, (1A, 1 B) 12 times, 1 A,
3 B, (1A, 1 B) to end.
2nd round K1 A, 2 B, (1 A, 1 B) 13 times, 1 A,
2 B, 2 A, (1 B, 1 A) to end.
3rd round Using A, K to end.
4th round As 3rd.
5th round K1 A, 2 C, (1 A, 1 C) 3 times, 3 A,
2 C, 5 A, 2 C, 3 A, (1 C, 1 A) 3 times, 2 C,
(1 A, 1 C) to end.
Cont in patt as now set, working the back of hand
from chart and palm of hand in one st of each
colour alternately throughout, until 9 patt rounds
have been worked.
Divide for thumb
10th round Patt 33 sts, sl next 10 sts on to a
holder, cast on 10 sts, patt to end.
Cont in patt until 33 rounds from chart have been
completed. Cont in A only until work measures
22cm ($8\frac{3}{4}in$) from beg.
Shape top
Next round (K1, sl 1, K1, psso, K27, K2 tog)
twice.
Next round K to end.
Next round (K1, sl 1, K1, psso, K25, K2 tog)
twice.
Cont dec 4 sts in this way on every foll alt round
until 32 sts rem, ending with a dec round. Dec as
before on next 3 rounds. 20 sts. Fold work in
half, placing dec at each side and graft sts tog.

Thumb
S1 st from holder on to a No. $2\frac{3}{4}$mm (*12*) needle.
Using A, K up 10 sts from cast on sts. Divide
these 20 sts between 3 needles. Cont working in
rounds of st st (every round K) until thumb
measures 6cm ($2\frac{1}{4}in$) from beg.
Shape top
Next round K2, *K2 tog, K1, rep from * to end.
Next round K to end.
Next round *K2 tog, rep from * to end.
Break off yarn, thread through rem sts, draw up
and fasten off.

Mitts left hand
Work to match right mitt, reversing position of
thumb as foll:
10th round Patt 54 sts, sl next 10 sts on to a
holder, cast on 10 sts.

To make up
Press as given for scarf on WS of work with
warm iron.
This beautiful Fair Isle set will make a colourful
addition to your winter wardrobe. Try knitting it
in a different colour combination for a new effect.

Baby bag

Sizes
To fit 45.5[51]cm (*18[20]in*) chest
Length from centre back, 62[63.5]cm (*24½[25]in*)
including bottom insertion
Sleeve seam, 18[20.5]cm (*7[8]in*)
Width around hood, 40.5cm (*16in*)
The figures in brackets[] refer to the 51cm (*20in*)
size only

Tension
28 sts and 36 rows to 10cm (*3.9in*) over st st
worked on No. $3\frac{1}{4}$mm (*10*) needles

Materials
6[7] × 25grm balls Emu Scotch Superwash 4 ply
in main shade, A
1[1] ball each of contrast colours, B and C
1[2] balls of contrast colour, D
10[11] balls of contrast colour, E
1[1] ball of contrast colour, F
One pair No. $3\frac{1}{4}$mm (*10*) needles
One pair No. $2\frac{3}{4}$mm (*12*) needles
One No. 2.00 (ISR) crochet hook
1 × 50[55]cm (*20[22]in*) zip fastener
2 buttons

Lining
Using No. $3\frac{1}{4}$mm (*10*) needles and E, cast on
160[174] sts and work in one piece to underarm.
Beg with a K row work in st st, K first and last
st on every row until work measures 48cm (*19in*)
from beg, ending with a P row.
Divide for armholes
Next row K34[37], cast off 12 sts, K68[76], cast
off 12 sts, K34[37].
Complete left front first. P 1 row. Dec one st at
armhole edge on next and every alt row until
30[33] sts rem. Cont without shaping until
armhole measures 7[8]cm ($2\frac{3}{4}[3\frac{1}{4}]in$) from beg,
ending at neck edge.
Shape neck
Cast off 6[7] sts at beg of next row. Dec one st
at neck edge on every row until 17[19] sts rem.
Cont without shaping until armhole measures
10[11.5]cm ($4[4\frac{1}{2}]in$) from beg, ending at armhole
edge.
Shape shoulder
Cast off at beg of next and every alt row 6 sts
twice and 5[7] sts once.
With WS of work facing, rejoin yarn to sts for
back, P to end. Dec one st at each end of next
and every alt row until 60[66] sts rem. Cont
without shaping until armholes measure same as

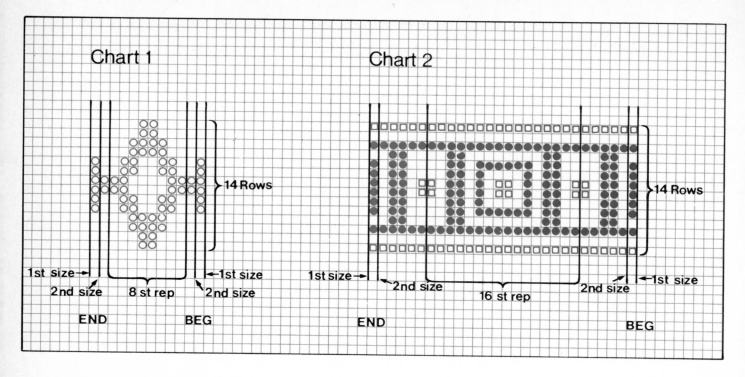

left front to shoulder, ending with a P row.

Shape shoulders
Cast off at beg of next and every row 6 sts 4 times, 5[7] sts twice and 26[28] sts once.
With WS of work facing, rejoin yarn to rem sts, P to end. Complete right front to match left front, reversing shaping.

Sleeves
Using No. 3¼mm (*10*) needles and E, cast on 58[62] sts. Beg with a K row work in st st until sleeve measures 16.5[19]cm (*6½[7½]in*) from beg, or required length to underarm, ending with a P row.

Shape top
Cast off 6 sts at beg of next 2 rows. Dec one st at each end of next and every alt row until 30 sts rem, then at each end of every row until 18 sts rem. Cast off.

Hood
Using No. 3¼mm (*10*) needles and E, cast on 114 sts. Beg with a K row work 56[62] rows st st. Cast off.

Bottom insertion
Using No. 3¼mm (*10*) needles and E, cast on 53[60] sts. Beg with a K row work in st st, inc one st at each end of 2nd and every row until there are 75[82] sts. Work 6 rows without shaping. Dec one st at each end of next and every row until 53[60] sts rem.
Cast off.

To make up
Press each piece under a damp cloth with a warm iron. Join shoulder and sleeve seams. Set in sleeves. Join back seam of hood. St hood to neck of lining, beg and ending 1cm (*½in*) from front edges and gathering hood slightly to fit back of neck. St bottom insertion into position at lower edge.

Pram bag
Using No. 3¼mm (*10*) needles and A, cast on 160[174] sts and work in one piece to underarm. Beg with a K row and keeping 2 sts at each end in g st on every row, work 14 rows st st. ** Work in patt from chart 1. Using A work 4 rows st st. Work in patt from chart 2. Using A work 4 rows st st. Work in patt from chart 3. Using A work 4 rows st st. Work in patt from chart 4. Using A work 4 rows st st. Work in patt from chart 5. Using A work 3 rows st st. Work in patt from chart 6. Using A work 4 rows st st. Rep from ** and complete as given for lining.

Sleeves
Check required length of sleeve from lining and exact patt row on which sleeve will beg to ensure that patt matches at underarm. Work as given for lining.

Cuffs
Using No. 2¾mm (*12*) needles, A and with RS of lower edge of sleeve facing, K up 44[46] sts. Work 10 rows K1, P1 rib. Cast off in rib.

Hood

Using No. 3¼mm (10) needles and A, cast on 114 sts. Beg with a K row work 12[14] rows st st. Work in patt from chart 1. Using A work 4[6] rows st st. Work in patt from chart 2. Using A only, complete as given for lining.

Bottom insertion

Using A, work as given for lining.

Chin strap

Using No. 3¼mm (10) needles and A, cast on 7 sts. K4 rows g st, inc one st at each end of 2nd and every row.
Next row (buttonhole row) K5, cast off 3 sts, K to end.

Next row K2, P3 cast on 3 sts, P3, K2.
Beg with a K row, cont in st st keeping 2 sts at each end in g st, and work 24[28] rows. Make buttonhole as before. K 4 rows g st, dec one st at each end of first 3 rows. Cast off.
Using E, make another piece in same way.

To make up

Press and make up as given for lining. With WS facing, insert lining into pram bag. St sleeve lining above cuff. Using No. 2.00 (ISR) hook, A and with RS of work facing, beg at lower edge of left front and work one row crab st up left front, round hood and down right front, working in dc from left to right instead of from right to left through both thicknesses of bag and lining. Sew

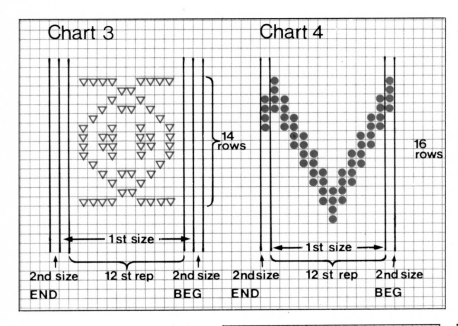

KEY □ – A   ● – D
    ○ – B   ▽ – E
    ▫ – C   ▲ – F

2 sts in garter st in A are worked before and after — Beg and End of Fair Isle pattern

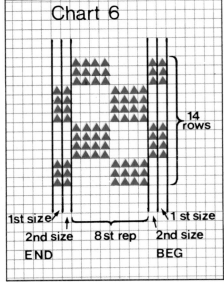

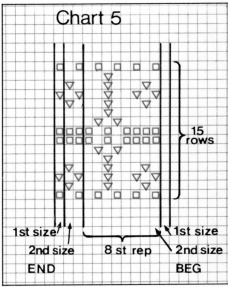

in zipper to come to top of neck, joining seam below zipper, if necessary. Sew on button to each side of neck edge. Join 2 chin strap pieces tog. Using all colors, make a pom-pon and sew to center of chin strap. Button chin strap to bunting.

Jacket with Fair Isle yoke

This traditional Fair Isle jacket features a round yoke and is buttoned to the neck. The Fair Isle pattern has been carefully planned to allow for the yoke shaping and authentic Scotch yarn and colors have been used.

Jacket with Fair Isle yoke
Sizes
Directions are to fit 34 inch bust.
Changes for 36, 38 and 40 inch bust are in brackets [].
Length to shoulder, 25½[26 : 26¼ : 26¾] inches.
Sleeve seam, 17[17¼ : 17¾ : 18¼] inches.

Gauge
28 sts and 36 rows to 4 inches over st st worked on No. 3 needles.

Materials
6[7 : 7 : 8]×1 oz balls Reynolds Gleneagles in main color, A
1 ball each of contrast colors, B. C. D. E. F. G and H
One pair No. 3 needles
One pair No. 1 needles
One No. 3 circular needle
8 buttons.

Back
Using No. 1 needles and A, cast on 139[147 : 155 : 163] sts.
1st row K1, *P1, K1, rep from * to end.
2nd row P1, *K1, P1, rep from * to end.
Rep these 2 rows 3 times more. Change to No. 3 needles. Beg with a K row cont in st st until work measures 3 inches from beg, ending with a P row.
Shape sides
Next row K1, K2 tog, K to last 3 sts, sl 1, K1, psso, K1.
Cont dec in this way at each end of every foll 16th row until 123[131 : 139 : 147] sts rem. Cont without shaping until work measures 18¼ inches from beg, ending with a P row.
Shape armholes
Bind off 6 sts at beg of next 2 rows.
Next row K1, K2 tog, K to last 3 sts, sl 1, K1, psso, K1.
Next row P to end.
Cont dec in this way on next and foll alt rows 1[3 : 5 : 7] times, ending with a P row. 107[111 : 115 : 119] sts.
Shape yoke
**1st row K1, K2 tog, K19[21 : 23 : 25] sts, turn.
2nd and every alt row Sl 1, P to end.
3rd row K1, K2 tog, K15[17 : 19 : 21], turn.
5th row K1, K2 tog, K12[14 : 16 : 18], turn.
7th row K1, K2 tog, K9[11 : 13 : 15], turn.
9th row K1, K2 tog, K7[9 : 11 : 13], turn.
Cont dec one st at armhole edge in this way and work one st less at inside edge on every alt row 3[4 : 5 : 6] times more, ending with a P row. **.
Break off yarn.
With RS of work facing, sl first 77[78 : 79 : 80] sts on to right hand needle, rejoin yarn to rem sts, K to last 3 sts, sl 1, K1, psso, K1.
1st row P18[20 : 22 : 24], turn.

1st row P18[20:22:24], turn.
2nd and every alt row Sl 1, K to last 3 sts, sl 1, K1, psso, K1.
3rd row P15[17:19:21], turn.
5th row P12[14:16:18], turn.
7th row P10[12:14:16], turn.
Complete to match first side, ending with a K row. Leave rem 91[93:95:97] sts on holder.

Left front

Using No. 2¾mm (*12*) needles and A, cast on 69[73:77:81] sts. Work 8 rows K1, P1 rib as given for back, inc one st at end of last row. 70[74:78: 82] sts. Change to No. 3¼mm (*10*) needles. Beg with a K row cont in st st until work measures 7.5cm (*3in*) from beg, ending with a P row.
Shape side
Next row K1, K2 tog, K to end.
Cont dec in this way at side edge on every foll 16th row until 62[66:70:74] sts rem. Cont without shaping until work measures same as back to underarm, ending with a P row.
Shape armhole
Cast off 6 sts at beg of next row.
Next row P to end.
Next row K1, K2 tog, K to end.
Cont dec in this way on every foll alt row 1[3:5:7] times in all, ending with a P row.

54[56:58:60] sts.
Shape yoke
Work as given for back from ** to **. Leave rem 46[47:48:49] sts on a holder.

Right front

Work as given for left front, reversing shaping.

Sleeves

Using No. 2¾mm (*12*) needles and A, cast on 55[57:59:61] sts. Work 5cm (*2in*) K1, P1 rib as given for back, ending with a 2nd row and inc one st at each end of last row. 57[59:61:63] sts. Change to No. 3¼mm (*10*) needles. Beg with a K row cont in st st inc one st at each end of 9th and every foll 8th row until there are 87[91:95:99] sts. Cont without shaping until work measures 43[44:45:46]cm (*17[17¼:17¾:18¼]in*) from beg, ending with a P row.
Shape top
Cast off 6 sts at beg of next 2 rows.
Next row K1, K2 tog, K to last 3 sts, sl 1, K1, psso, K1.
Next row P to end.
Cont dec in this way on next and every foll alt row until 55[53:51:49] sts rem, ending with a P row. Leave sts on holder.

Yoke

Using No. 3¼mm (*10*) circular Twin Pin, A and with RS of right front facing, K across all sts on holders, K2 tog at each seam. 289 sts.
Next row P to end.
Beg with a K row work 22 rows Fair Isle patt from Chart 1.
Next row Using A, K4, *K2 tog, K7, rep from * to last 6 sts, K2 tog, K4. 257 sts.
Beg with a P row work 2nd - 4th rows from Chart 1.
Next row Using A, K3, *K2 tog, K6, rep from * to last 6 sts, K2 tog, K4. 225 sts.
Beg with a P row work 15 rows Fair Isle patt from Chart 11.
Next row Using A, K3, *K2 tog, K5, rep from * to last 5 sts, K2 tog, K3. 193 sts.
Rep 2nd - 4th rows from Chart 1 once more. Cont with A only.
Next row K3, *K2 tog, K3, rep from * to end. 155 sts.
Beg with a P row work 3 rows st st.
Next row K3, *K2 tog, K2, rep from * to end. 117 sts.
P one row. Leave rem sts on holder.

Left front band

Using No. 2¾mm (*12*) needles and A, cast on 11 sts. Work in K1, P1 rib as given for back until

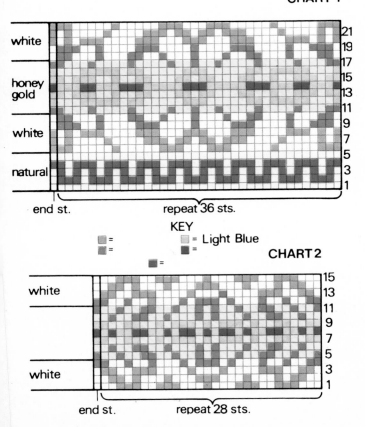

CHART 1

white

honey gold

white

natural

end st.   repeat 36 sts.

KEY

▨ =
▨ =
▨ =   ▨ = Light Blue
            ▨ =

CHART 2

white

white

end st.   repeat 28 sts.

band, slightly stretched fits up left front to neck edge, ending with a 2nd row. Leave sts on holder. Mark positions for 8 buttons, first to come in centre of welt and last in neckband approx 1cm ($\frac{3}{8}in$) above sts on holder with the others evenly spaced between.

Right front band
Work to match left front band, making buttonholes to correspond with markers as foll:
Next row (RS) Rib 4, cast off 3, rib to end.
Next row Rib to end, casting on 3 sts above those cast off in previous row.

Neckband
Using No. 2$\frac{3}{4}$mm (*12*) needles and A, rib across 10 right front sts on holder, K next st tog with first st of neck edge, rib across neck sts to last st, K last st tog with first st of left front band, rib across 10 rem sts. 137 sts. Work 15 rows K1, P1 rib making buttonholes as before on 4th and 12th rows. Cast off in rib.

To make up
Press under a damp cloth with a warm iron. Join raglan seams. Join side and sleeve seams. Fold neckband in half to WS and sl st into position. Sew on buttons to correspond with buttonholes. Press seams.

Super sleeveless slipover

Sizes
To fit 86.5[91.5:96.5:101.5]cm (*34[36:38:40]in*) bust/chest
Length to shoulder, 61[62:66:67.5]cm (*24[24$\frac{1}{2}$: 26:26$\frac{1}{2}$]in*)
The figures in brackets [] refer to the 91.5 (*36*), 96.5 (*38*) and 101.5cm (*40in*) sizes respectively

Tension
26 sts and 32 rows to 10cm (*3.9in*) over patt worked on No. 3$\frac{3}{4}$mm (*9*) needles

Materials
5[5:6:6] × 40grm balls Wendy Marina Double

Crepe in main shade, A
5[6:7:8] × 20grm balls of Wendy Random Courtelle Double Crepe in contrast colour, B
One pair No. 3$\frac{3}{4}$mm (*9*) needles
One pair No. 3mm (*11*) needles

Back
Using No. 3mm (*11*) needles and A, cast on 113[121:129:137] sts.
1st row K1, *P1, K1, rep from * to end.
2nd row P1, *K1, P1, rep from * to end.
Rep these 2 rows 11 times more. Change to No. 3$\frac{3}{4}$mm (*9*) needles. Beg with a K row cont in st st, working in patt from chart, until work measures 43[43:45.5:45.5]cm (*17[17:18:18]in*) from beg, ending with a WS row.
Shape armholes
Keeping patt correct, cast off 6 sts at beg of next 2 rows. Dec one st at each end of next 8[9:10:11] rows. 85[91:97:103] sts. Cont in patt without shaping until armholes measure 18[19:20.5:21.5] cm (*7[7$\frac{1}{2}$:8:8$\frac{1}{2}$]in*) from beg, ending with a WS row.
Shape shoulders
Cast off at beg of next and every row 8[9:9:10] sts twice, 8[9:10:10] sts twice, 9[9:10:11] sts twice and 35[37:39:41] sts once.

Front
Work as given for back until front measures 40.5[40.5:43:43]cm (*16[16:17:17]in*) from beg, ending with a WS row.
Divide for neck
Next row Patt 56[60:64:68] sts, cast off one st, patt to end.
Complete this side first. Work 1 row. Dec one st at neck edge on next and every foll alt row 5[6:7:8] times in all, then on every foll 3rd row 12 times in all, *at the same time* shape armhole when work measures same as back to underarm, ending at armhole edge.
Shape armhole
Cast off 6 sts at beg of next row. Dec one st at armhole edge on next 8[9:10:11] rows. Keeping armhole edge straight, cont shaping at front neck until 25[27:29:31] sts rem. Cont without shaping until armhole measures same as back to shoulder, ending at armhole edge.
Shape shoulder
Cast off at beg of next and every alt row 8[9:9:10] sts once, 8[9:10:10] sts once and 9[9:10:11] sts once.
With WS of work facing, rejoin yarn to rem sts and patt to end. Complete to match first side, reversing shaping.

Neckband
Join right shoulder seam. Using No. 3mm (*11*)

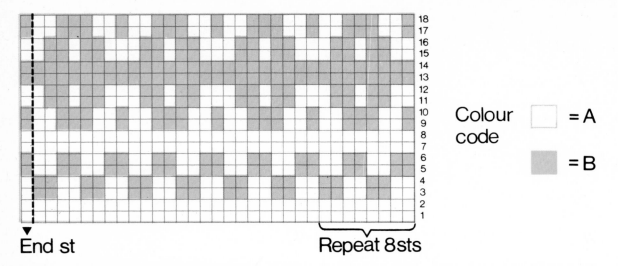

needles, A and with RS of work facing, K up 64[66:68:70] sts down left front neck, K up one st at centre front and mark with coloured thread, K up 64[66:68:70] sts up right front neck and 34[36:38:40] sts across back neck. 163[169:175: 181] sts.

1st row Work in K1, P1 rib to one st before centre marked st, P3 tog, rib to end.

2nd row Rib to one st before centre marked st, K3 tog, rib to end.

Rep last 2 rows 3 times more, then work first row once more.

Cast off in rib.

Armbands
Join left shoulder and neckband seam. Using No. 3mm (*11*) needles, A and with RS of work facing, K up 102[106:110:114] sts round armhole. Work 9 rows K1, P1 rib. Cast off in rib.

To make up
Press under a dry cloth with a warm iron. Join side seams.
Press seams.

Fair Isle variations

Scandinavian borders

The Scandinavian countries provide an endless source of what are loosely termed 'Fair Isle' designs, particularly variations of the delightful snowflake pattern. They are worked in the same way as the traditional Shetland designs but the patterns are usually bolder and the choice of colour is more distinctive.

From the middle European countries and further east, more intricate and colourful designs are introduced, often involving the use of three or more colours at a time. These beautiful fabrics, often based upon traditional carpet designs, feature floral or symmetrical patterns in rich, jewel colours.

To look effective, the samples given here should not be used as over-all patterns but as borders, pockets or cuff motifs.

Border pattern No. 1

This can either be worked as a horizontal or vertical border. For a horizontal border cast on multiples of 20 stitches plus 7 and work the 7 pattern rows from the chart. To work the border

vertically, turn the chart sideways and work over 7 stitches for 20 rows.

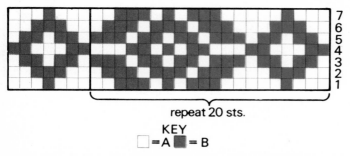

repeat 20 sts.

KEY
☐ = A ◼ = B

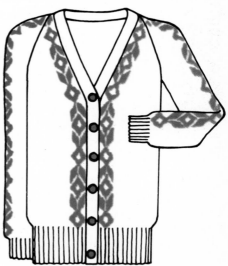

Border pattern No. 2

This pattern can also be worked horizontally or vertically. For a horizontal border cast on multiples of 10 stitches and complete the 21 rows from the chart. For a vertical border, turn the chart sideways and work over 21 stitches for 10 rows.

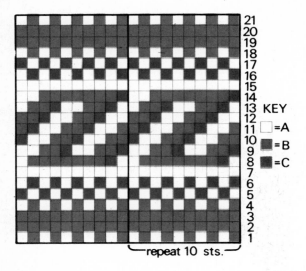

KEY

□ =A
▨ =B
■ =C

repeat 10 sts.

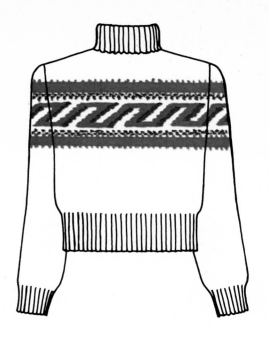

Border pattern No. 3

This pattern has a distinctly oriental appearance and can only be worked as a horizontal border.

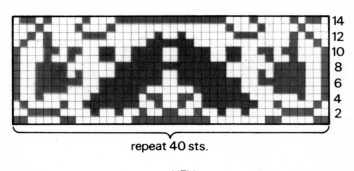

repeat 40 sts.

KEY

□ = A ■ = C
▨ = B ▨ = D

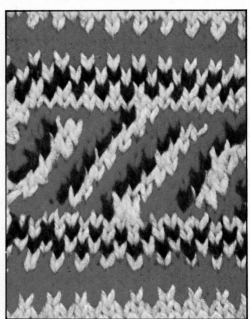

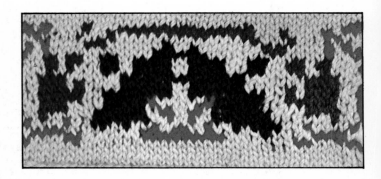

Snowflake pattern

This beautiful Scandinavian motif has many uses. It can be worked as a single pattern over 35 stitches, keeping additional stitches on either side in the background colour, to form a pocket or to highlight a sleeve just above the cuff. The design can also be worked as a horizontal or vertical border, over multiples of 35 stitches and 35 rows.

Star pattern
Another motif which can be used singly or as a horizontal border pattern.

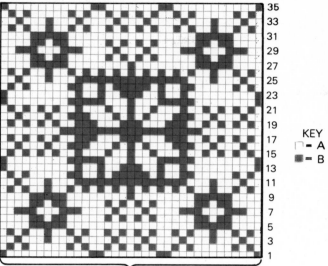

35
33
31
29
27
25
23
21
19
17
15
13
11
9
7
5
3
1

KEY
☐ = A
▨ = B

repeat 35 sts.

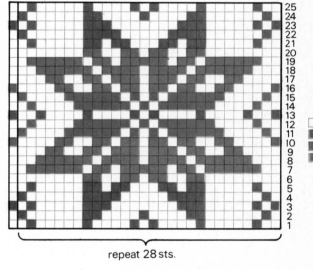

25
24
23
22
21
20
19
18
17
16
15
14
13
12
11
10
9
8
7
6
5
4
3
2
1

KEY
☐ = A
▨ = B
▨ = C
▨ = D

repeat 28 sts.

A star style

Sizes
To fit 86.5cm (*34in*) bust
Length to shoulder, 53.5cm (*21in*)

Tension
26 sts and 30 rows to 10cm (*3.9in*) over st st
worked on No. 3¾mm (*9*) needles

Materials
4 × 50grm balls of Patons Kismet
2 balls of contrast colour, B
One pair No. 3¾mm (*9*) needles
One pair No. 3¼mm (*10*) needles
Set of 4 No. 3¼mm (*10*) needles pointed at ends

Back
Using No. 3¼mm (*10*) needles and A, cast on 110
sts.
1st row K2, *P2, K2, rep from * to end.
2nd row P2, *K2, P2, rep from * to end.
Rep these 2 rows for 10cm (*4in*), ending with a
2nd row and dec one st in centre of last row.
109 sts. Change to No. 3¾mm (*9*) needles. **Beg
with a K row work 6 rows st st. Work 25 rows of
star patt from chart 1. **. Beg with a P row work
6 rows st st. Work 7 rows of heart patt from
chart 2, keeping sts at each end in A as shown.
Rep from ** to **, then work 3 rows st st.
Shape armholes
Cast off 7 sts at beg of next 2 rows. 95 sts. Dec
one st at each end of next row. Work 7 rows of
heart patt from chart 2, keeping patt correct in
line with previous one and dec one st at each end
of 2nd, 4th and 6th rows. Work 6 rows st st, dec
one st at each end of 1st, 3rd and 5th rows.
81 sts. Work 25 rows of star patt from chart 1,
keeping patt correct in line with previous one.
Break off B. Using A only, cont in st st until
armholes measure 18cm (*7in*) from beg, ending
with a P row.
Shape shoulder and neck
Next row Cast off 8 sts, K21, turn and leave rem
sts on holder.
Cast off at beg of next and every row 3 sts once,
8 sts once, 3 sts once and 7 sts once.
With RS of work facing, sl first 23 sts on to holder
and leave for centre back neck, rejoin yarn to rem
sts and K to end. Complete to match first side,
reversing shaping.

Front
Work as given for back until front measures same
as back to underarm, ending with a P row.

Shape armholes and divide for neck
Cast off 7 sts at beg of next 2 rows.
Next row K2 tog, K45, turn and leave rem sts
on holder.
Next row Working in heart patt from chart 2 to

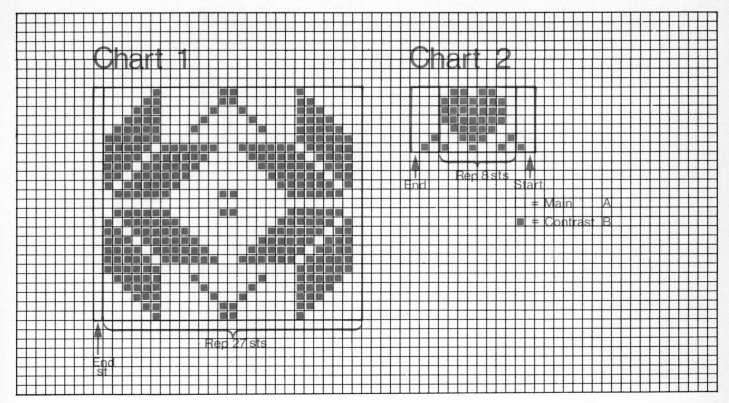

Chart 1

Chart 2

Rep 27 sts

End st

Rep 8 sts

End   Start

⊟ = Main   A
▣ = Contrast B

match back, P2 tog, P to end.

Cont in patt to match back, dec one st at armhole edge on next and foll 5 alt rows, *at the same time* dec one st at neck edge on every foll 3rd row until 23 sts rem. Cont without shaping until armhole measures same as back to shoulder, ending at armhole edge.

Shape shoulder

Cast off at beg of next and every alt row, 8 sts twice and 7 sts once.

With RS of work facing, sl first st on holder for centre front neck, rejoin yarn to rem sts, K to last 2 sts, K2 tog tbl. Complete to match first side, reversing shaping.

Neckband

Join shoulder seams. Using set of 4 No. 3¼mm (*10*) needles, A and with RS of work facing, K up 6 sts down right back neck, K across back neck sts on holder dec one st in centre, K up 6 sts up left back neck and 49 sts down left front neck, K centre front st from holder and K up 49 sts up right front neck. 133 sts.

Next round Work in K2, P2 rib to 2 sts before centre front st, K2 tog, P1, sl 1, K1, psso, work in K2, P2 rib to end.

Rep last round 5 times more. Cast off in rib still dec at centre front.

Armbands

Using No. 3¼mm (*10*) needles, A and with RS of work facing, K up 98 sts round armhole. Beg first row with P2, work 6 rows K2, P2 rib. Cast off in rib.

To make up

Press each piece under a dry cloth with a cool iron. Join side seams.
Press seams.

Mock Fair Isle and jersey

Although they look rather complicated, Fair Isle patterns are quite simple to work as they rarely use more than two colours in one row at a time. The beautiful, multi-coloured effects are achieved by varying the two combinations of colours.
A form of 'mock' Fair Isle, however, is even simpler to work as this only requires two colours throughout — a plain background colour and a random yarn used for the contrast colour. As the random yarn is worked, it changes its colour sequence to give a most striking effect.

Unlike striped patterns, where the colour is changed at the end of a row, two yarns will be in use during the course of a row. As only a few stitches are worked in one colour, the yarn not in use can be carried loosely across the back of the work until it is required, then twisted round the last colour before it is brought into use again.

Three 'mock' Fair Isle patterns

Any of the three charts shown here can be used to make this short sleeved jersey, as each pattern requires multiples of 8 stitches plus one.

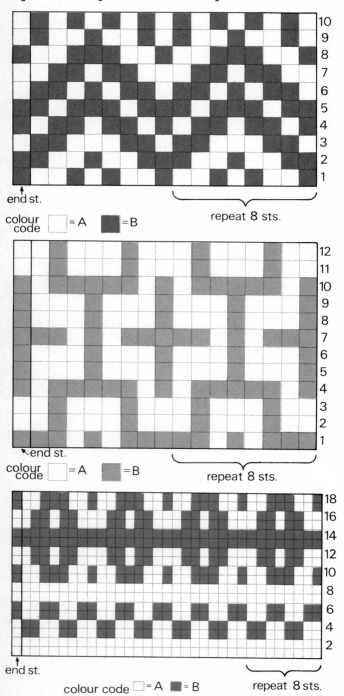

'Mock' Fair Isle jersey

Sizes

To fit 86.5[91.5:96.5:101.5]cm (*34[36:38:40]in*) bust

Length to shoulder, 61[62:66:67]cm (*24[24½:26: 26½]in*)

Sleeve seam, 10cm (*4in*)

The figures in brackets [] refer to the 91.5 (*36*), 96.5 (*38*) and 101.5cm (*40in*) sizes respectively

Tension

26 sts and 32 rows to 10cm (*3.9in*) over patt worked on No. 3¾mm (*9*) needles

Materials

7[7:8:8] × 40grm balls Wendy Marina Double Crepe in main shade, A

6[7:8:9] × 20grm balls Wendy Random Courtelle Double Crepe in contrast colour, B

One pair No. 3¾mm (*9*) needles

One pair No. 3mm (*11*) needles

Back

Using No. 3mm (*11*) needles and A, cast on
113[121:129:137] sts.
1st row K1, *P1, K1, rep from * to end.
2nd row P1, *K1, P1, rep from * to end.
Rep these 2 rows 11 times more. Change to
No. 3¾mm (*9*) needles. Beg with a K row cont in
st st, working in any patt from chart, until work
measures 43[43:45.5:45.5]cm (*17[17:18:18]in*)
from beg, ending with a WS row.
Shape armholes
Keeping patt correct, cast off 6[7:8:9] sts at beg
of next 2 rows. Dec one st at each end of next
8[9:10:11] rows. 85[89:93:97] sts. Cont in patt
without shaping until armholes measure
18[19:20.5:21.5]cm (*7[7½:8:8½]in*) from beg,
ending with a WS row.
Shape shoulders
Cast off at beg of next and every row 8[8:9:9] sts
twice, 8[9:9:9] sts twice and 9[9:9:10] sts twice.
Leave rem 35[37:39:41] sts on holder for back
neck.

Front

Work as given for back until armhole shaping has
been completed. 85[89:93:97] sts. Cont without
shaping until armholes measure 14[15:16.5:18] cm
(*5½[6:6½:7]in*) from beg, ending with a WS row.
Shape neck
Next row Patt 32[33:34:35], turn and leave rem
sts on holder.
Complete this side first. Dec one st at neck edge
on next and every row 7 times in all. 25[26:27:28]
sts. Cont without shaping until front matches back
to shoulder, ending at armhole edge.
Shape shoulder
Cast off at beg of next and every alt row 8[8:9:9]
sts once, 8[9:9:9] sts once and 9[9:9:10] sts once.
With RS of work facing, sl first 21[23:25:27] sts
on to holder for front neck, rejoin yarn to rem
sts and patt to end. Complete to match first side,
reversing shaping.

Short sleeves

Using No. 3mm (*11*) needles and A, cast on
81[89:89:97] sts. Work 12 rows rib as given for
back. Change to No. 3¾mm (*9*) needles. Beg with a
K row cont in st st, working in any patt from
chart and inc one st at each end of 3rd and every
foll 6th row, until there are 87[95:95:103] sts.
Cont without shaping until sleeve measures 10cm
(*4in*) from beg, ending with a WS row.
Shape top
Cast off 6[7:8:9] sts at beg of next 2 rows. Dec
one st at each end of next and every foll alt row
until 47[53:47:49] sts rem. Patt one row. Cast off
2 sts at beg of next 16[18:14:14] rows.

Cast off rem 15[17:19:21] sts.

Neckband

Join right shoulder seam. Using No. 3mm (*11*)
needles, A and with RS of work facing, K up 16
sts down left front neck, K across front neck sts
on holder, K up 15 sts up right front neck and K
across back neck sts on holder. 87[91:95:99] sts.
Work 12 rows rib as given for back. Cast off
loosely in rib.

To make up

Press under a dry cloth with a warm iron. Join
left shoulder and neckband seams. Set in sleeves.
Join side and sleeve seams. Press seams.

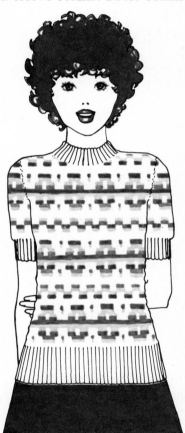

Mock Fair Isle dressing gown

The mock Fair Isle technique has been used for
this trendy cardigan dressing gown for a toddler.

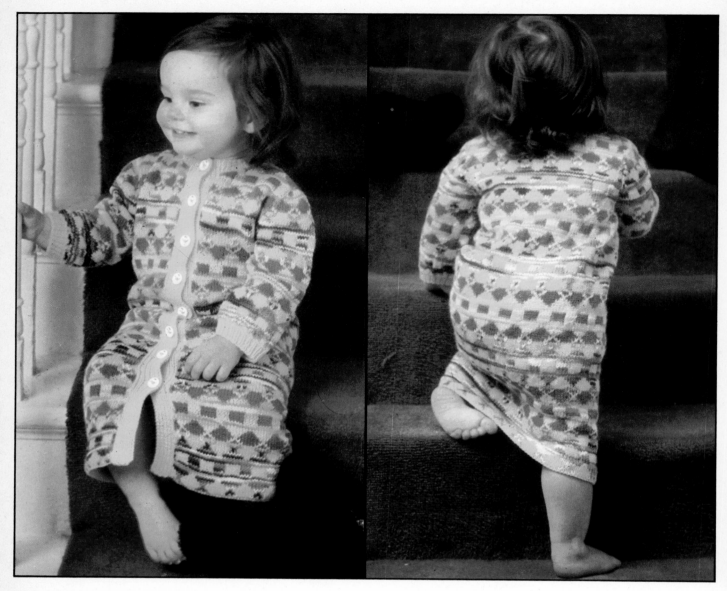

An even more interesting pattern has been achieved, however, by using a plain background with a contrasting random yarn for the first pattern repeat, then reversing the pattern by using a second random yarn as the background and a second plain colour for the contrast for the next repeat.

Dressing gown
Sizes
To fit 56[61]cm (*22[24]in*) chest
Length to shoulder, 56[61]cm (*22[24]in*)
Sleeve seam, 16.5[20.5]cm (*6½[8]in*)
The figures in brackets [] refer to the 61cm (*24in*) size only

Tension
28 sts and 36 rows to 10cm (*3.9in*) over patt worked on No. 3¼mm (*10*) needles

Materials
3[4] × 20grm balls of Sirdar Wash'n'wear 4 ply Crepe in 1st contrast, A
3[3] × 25grm balls of Sirdar Multi 4 ply in 2nd contrast, B
2[2] × 20 grm balls of Sirdar Wash'n'wear 4 ply Crepe in 3rd contrast, C
2[3] × 25 grm balls Sirdar Multi 4 ply in 4th contrast, D
One pair No. 3¼mm (*10*) needles
One pair No. 2¾mm (*12*) needles
8 buttons

Back and fronts
Using No. 2¾mm (*12*) needles and A, cast on 162[175] sts and work in one piece to underarm.
Beg with a K row work 9 rows st st.
Next row K all sts tbl to form hemline.
Change to No. 3¼mm (*10*) needles. Beg with a K

row cont in st st, join in B and work ** 22 rows from chart using A and B. Break off A and B. Join in C and D and work 22 rows from chart, using C for A and D for B. **. Cont in patt from ** to ** until work measures 43[47.5]cm (17[18¾]in) from hemline, ending with a WS row.

Divide for armholes
Next row Patt 37 [39] sts, cast off 6[8] sts, patt 76[81] sts, cast off 6[8] sts, patt 37[39] sts. Complete left front first. Keeping patt correct, dec one st at armhole edge on every row until 31[32] sts rem. Cont without shaping until armhole measures 9[9.5]cm (3½[3¾]in) from beg, ending at neck edge.

Shape neck
Cast off 5 sts at beg of next row. Dec one st at neck edge on every row until 20[20] sts rem. Cont without shaping until armhole measures 11.5[12]cm (4½[4¾]in) from beg, ending at armhole edge.

Shape shoulder
Cast off at beg of next and foll alt row 10 sts twice.
With WS of work facing, rejoin yarn to sts for back. Keeping patt correct, dec one st at each end of every row until 64[67] sts rem. Cont without shaping until armholes measure same as left front to shoulder, ending with a WS row.

Shape shoulders
Cast off at beg of next and every row 10 sts 4 times and 24[27] sts once.
With WS of work facing, rejoin yarn to rem sts and complete right front to match left front, reversing shaping.

Sleeves
Using No. 2¾mm (12) needles and A, cast on 44[48] sts. Work 10 rows K1, P1 rib, inc 19[15] sts evenly across last row. 63[63] sts. Change to No. 3¼mm (10) needles. Cont in patt as given for back until sleeve measures 16.5[20.5]cm (6½[8]in) from beg, taking care to beg with a patt row and colour which will enable sleeve seam to be completed on same row as back and fronts at underarm, ending with a WS row.

Shape top
Cast off 3[4] sts at beg of next 2 rows. Dec one st at each end of next and every alt row until 39[41] sts rem, then at each end of every row until 27 sts rem. Dec 2 sts at each end of every row until 11 sts rem. Cast off.

Button band
Using No. 2¾mm (12) needles and A, cast on 12 sts. Work in K1, P1 rib until band is long enough, when slightly stretched, to fit from hemline to beg of neck shaping. Leave sts on holder. St button band in place on left front for a girl and right front for a boy from hemline to neck. Mark positions for 8 buttons on button band, the first to come in neckband with 7 more evenly spaced at 5cm (2in) intervals, measured from base of previous buttonhole.

Buttonhole band
Work as given for button band, making buttonholes as markers are reached, as foll:
1st row (buttonhole row) Rib 5 sts, cast off 2, rib to end.
2nd row Rib to end, casting on 2 sts above those cast off in previous row.
Leave sts on holder.

Neckband
Join shoulder seams. St buttonhole band in place. Using No. 2¾mm (12) needles, A and with RS of work facing, sl 12 sts of band on to needle, K up 59[63] sts evenly around neck then rib across rem sts on holder. Work 1 row K1, P1 rib. Make buttonhole as before on next 2 rows. Work 3 more rows rib. Cast off in rib.

To make up
Press each piece under a damp cloth with a warm iron. Join sleeve seams. Set in sleeves. Press seams. Turn hem to WS at lower edge and sl st down. Sew on buttons.

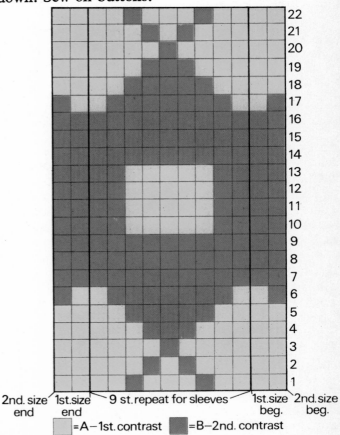

2nd. size end | 1st.size end | 9 st.repeat for sleeves | 1st.size beg. | 2nd.size beg.

☐ =A−1st. contrast ■ =B−2nd. contrast

Jacquard and collage

Whereas traditional Fair Isle knitting normally uses only two colours in any one row, jacquard, collage and patchwork knitting are all forms of the same technique, where more than two colours are used at a time in any one pattern row. These designs are best worked in stocking stitch against a stocking stitch background, although collage knitting may also combine many different stitches to great effect.

Unlike Fair Isle knitting, this means that this method is very clumsy and untidy to work, when more than one strand has to be carried across the back of the work until required again. It is possible to work a small repeating jacquard design in this way, carrying the yarn not in use loosely across the back of the work but this does, inevitably, mean variance in tension against the main fabric. When working in this way, it is therefore advisable to change to one size larger needles to work the jacquard pattern, reverting to the correct needle size to work the main pattern. The correct method of working all large, multi-coloured patterns, motifs, wide vertical stripes and patchwork designs, is to use small, separate balls of yarn for each colour. In this way a fabric of single thickness is formed, without any strands of yarn across the back of the work. These patterns are usually worked from a chart, just as Fair Isle knitting, with each different colour coded with a symbol.

Use of bobbins

Before beginning to knit, wind all the colours which are required into small, separate balls round a bobbin. These are easy to handle and hang at the back of the work, keeping each colour free from tangles.

To make a bobbin

Use a stiff piece of cardboard and cut to shape as shown in diagram, having a slit at the top of each bobbin. Wind the yarn round the centre of the bobbin with the working end passing through the slits.

Joining in each new colour

The next important point to remember is that knitting patterns of a geometric or random shape, such as diamonds or flower motifs, as opposed to straight vertical stripes, require the colour to be changed by means of looping the two yarns round each other, on a right side row, to avoid gaps in the knitting. On the return purl row it is not so essential to loop the yarns round each other, as the purl stitch will probably encroach into the pattern sequence and the yarns will automatically be looped. Vertical bands of colour, however, must be looped on every row, as there will be no encroaching stitch to form a natural link in either direction.

To loop yarns on a knit row

Keep each ball of yarn at the back of the work until it is required, knit the last stitch in the first colour, then take this end of yarn over the next colour to be used and drop it, pick up the next colour under this strand of yarn, take it over the strand ready to knit the next stitch.

To loop yarns on a purl row

Keep each ball of yarn at the front of work until it is required, purl the last stitch in the first colour, then take this end of yarn over the next colour to be used and drop it, pick up the next colour under this strand of yarn, take it over the strand ready to purl the next stitch.

Jacquard and Collage knitting

Jacquard and collage knitting provide tremendous scope for interesting all-over patterned fabrics, or as a single motif incorporated into an otherwise plain background.

The examples shown here should be worked with small separate balls of yarn, twisting the yarns at the back of the work when changing colour.

Motifs

Almost any shape or design can be used as a separate jacquard motif, but if you are working out your own pattern it must be charted out on graph paper first, allowing one square for each stitch and one line of squares for each row. Code each different colour with a symbol and make a colour key of these symbols.

If you do not want to make your own designs, use an embroidery chart, such as given for cross stitch embroidery, and adapt this to suit your own colour scheme, again coding each different colour with a symbol.

Butterfly motif

This motif is worked in five contrasting colours against a plain background, making six colours in all. Each motif requires a total of 28 stitches and 34 rows to complete.

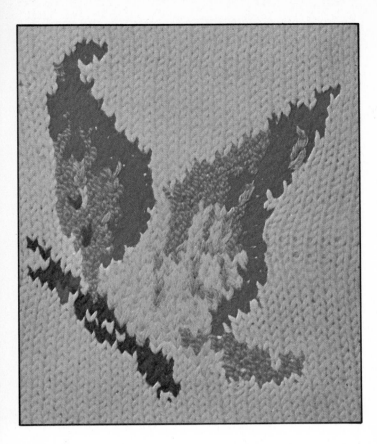

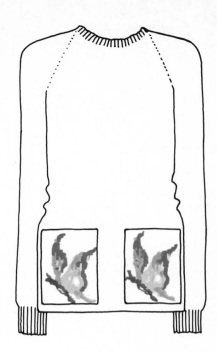

Heart motif

Here again, five contrast colours have been used against a plain background, making a total of six. Each motif requires a total of 35 stitches and 32 rows to complete.

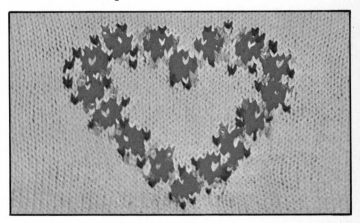

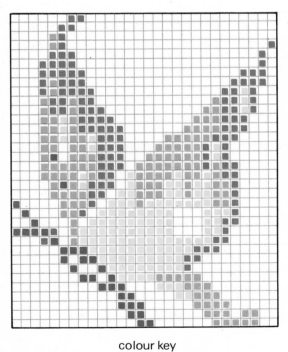

colour key

■=B ■=C □=D ■=E ▨=F

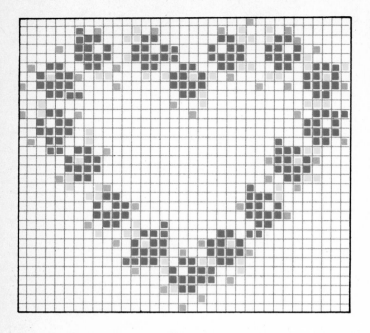

colour key

□=B ▦=C ☐=D ▨=E ☐=F

Multi-coloured collage pattern

This design can be worked with as many colours
as you require, varying the sequence to ensure
that you do not use the same colours next to each

other. Cast on a number of stitches divisible by
10, using the main colour. The sample shown here
has been worked over 50 stitches with five
colours.

1st row (RS) K10 sts in each of 5 colours.
2nd row Using same colours, P10 sts in each of
5 colours.
Rep 1st and 2nd rows once more.
5th row Varying colour sequence as required, K1
with contrast colour, K8 with original colour, *K2
with next contrast colour, K8 with original colour,
rep from * to last st, K1 with last contrast colour.

6th row P2 with same contrast colour, *P6, with
original colour, P4 with same contrast colour, rep
from * to last 8 sts, P6 with original colour, P2
with same contrast colour.
7th row K3 with same contrast colour, *K4 with
original colour, K6 with same contrast colour, rep
from * to last 7 sts, K4 with original colour, K3
with same contrast colour.
8th row P4 with same contrast colour, *P2 with
original colour, break off original colour, P8 with
same contrast colour, rep from * to last 6 sts,
P2 with original colour, break off original colour,
P4 with same contrast colour.
9th row K5 with same contrast colour, keeping
colour sequence correct as now set, K10 sts with
each colour to last 5 sts, K5 sts with same colour.
10th row P as 9th row.
Rep 9th and 10th rows 3 times more.
17th row K4 sts with original colour as now set,
*K2 sts with next contrast colour, K8 sts with
original colour as now set, rep from * to last 6
sts, K2 with next contrast colour, K4 with original
colour as now set.
18th row P3 sts with original colour, *P4 with
same contrast colour, P6 with original colour, rep
from * to last 7 sts, P4 with same contrast colour,
P3 with original colour.
19th row K2 with original colour, *K6 with same
contrast colour, K4 with original colour, rep from
* to last 8 sts, K6 with same contrast colour, K2
with original colour.
20th row P1 with original colour, break off
original colour, *P8 with same contrast colour,
P2 with original colour, break off original colour,
rep from * to last 9 sts, P8 with same contrast
colour, P1 with original colour, break off original
colour.
21st row Keeping colour sequence correct as now
set, work as given for 1st row.
22nd row As 2nd.
23rd row As 1st.
24th row As 2nd.
These 24 rows form the pattern.

Collage pram cover
Size
56cm (*22in*) wide by 81.5cm (*32in*) long

Tension
18 sts and 22 rows to 10cm (*3.9in*) over st st
worked on No. 5mm (*6*) needles

Materials
5 × 50grm balls Sirdar Pullman in main shade, A
1 ball each of 7 contrast colours, B, C, D, E, F,
G and H
One pair No. 5mm (*6*) needles

Pram cover centre
Using No. 5mm (*6*) needles and A, cast on 80 sts. Work in multi-coloured collage pattern until work measures 71cm (*28in*) from beg, ending with a 12th patt row. Cast off.

Border
Using No. 5mm (*6*) needles and A, cast on 100 sts. K16 rows g st.
Next row K10 sts, cast off 80 sts, K10 sts. Complete this side first. Cont in g st until band fits along side edge of cover, ending at inside edge. Break off yarn. Leave sts on holder.
With WS of work facing, rejoin yarn to rem 10 sts and complete to match first side, ending at outside edge. Do not break off yarn.
Next row K across first 10 sts, turn and cast on 80 sts, K across rem 10 sts on holder. 100 sts. K 16 rows g st. Cast off loosely.

To make up
Press centre only under a damp cloth with a warm iron. With RS facing, sew border round outer edge of centre.
Press seams.

Pretty patchwork dungarees

Completely random patchwork fabrics are worked in the same way as collage patterns, using separate balls of yarn for each colour.
Each patch can be worked over any even number of stitches, or as many number of rows required, and as each patch is completed it is not necessary to cast off, as you simply carry on with the next patch and colour sequence. The exciting part of this technique comes in arranging the sequence of patches, as no two knitters will work either the same colour or patch in identical order, so each sample has a completely original appearance.

The required number of stitches may be cast on to work two, three or more patches side by side to give an overall fabric, or single patches can be worked in separate strips to the required length and then sewn together. The latter method means that shaping can be achieved on each side of the strips, to achieve a well-fitting skirt or the delightful patchwork dungarees shown here.

Patchwork samples

In all the examples given here the first, or main colour, is coded as A, the next colour as B, the next colour as C and so on and a total of six colours have been used. Once you have decided which colours you would like to use, make a note of the sequence in which you are going to work them so that when you have to pick up contrast colour E you will know immediately to which colour this refers.

These samples have been worked over 28 stitches, allowing 30 rows for each patch. Cast on with A.

1st patch
1st row Using A, K to end.
2nd row Using A, P to end.
Rep these 2 rows 14 times more, using each colour in turn to form stripes. 30 rows.

2nd patch
1st row K14 B, 14 C.
2nd row P14 C, 14 B.
Rep these 2 rows 6 times more.
15th row Using D, K to end.
16th row Using D, P to end.
17th row K14 E, 14 F.
18th row P14 F, 14 E.
Rep last 2 rows 6 times more. 30 rows.

3rd patch
1st row Using A, K to end.
2nd row Using A, P to end.
Rep these 2 rows 4 times more.
11th row K10 B, 8 C, 10 D.
12th row P10 D, 8 C, 10 B.
Rep last 2 rows 9 times more. 30 rows.

4th patch
1st row Using E, K to end.
2nd row Using E, P to end.
Rep these 2 rows 14 times more. 30 rows.
Each time you work a repeat of this patch, use a different colour.

5th patch
1st row K12 F, 4 A, 12 B.
2nd row P12 B, 4 A, 12 F.
Rep these 2 rows 5 times more.

13th row Using C, K to end.
14th row Using C, P to end.
Rep last 2 rows twice more.
19th row K12 D, 4 E, 12 F.
20th row P12 F, 4 E, 12 D.
Rep last 2 rows 5 times more. 30 rows.

Dungarees
Size
Length to back waist, 45.5cm (*18in*)
Inside leg, 25 5cm (*10in*)

Tension
30 sts and 38 rows to 10cm (*3.9in*) over st st worked on No. 3¼mm (*10*) needles

Materials
2 × 25grm balls of Emu Scotch Superwash 4 ply in main shade, A
1 ball each of 5 contrast colours, B, C, D, E and F
One pair No. 3¼mm (*10*) needles
2 buttons
Waist length of elastic

Right front leg
**Using No. 3¼mm (*10*) needles and A, cast on 28 sts. Beg with a K row work 7 rows st st.
Next row Using A, K all sts tbl to form hemline. Work 1st, 2nd, 3rd, 4th and 5th patches, dec one st at beg of 9th and every foll 4th row 4 times in all, noting that less sts will be worked in first block of colour. 24 sts. Cont in patt without shaping until 60th patt row has been completed. **. Keeping patt correct, inc one st at beg of next and every foll 4th row 6 times in all, noting that extra sts will be worked in first block of colour. 30 sts. Cont without shaping until 82nd patt row has been completed.

Shape crotch
Cast off 2 sts at beg of next row. Work 1 row. Dec one st at beg of next and foll alt rows 4 times in all. 24 sts. Cont without shaping until 142nd patt row has been completed. Using A, work 8 rows K1, P1 rib. Cast off loosely in rib.

Right side leg
Using No. 3¼mm (*10*) needles and A, cast on 32 sts. Work hem as given for right front leg. Work 4th, 5th, 2nd, 1st and 3rd patches, shaping dart on 9th row as foll:
1st dec row Patt 14 sts, K2 tog, sl 1, K1, psso, patt 14 sts.
Work 3 rows without shaping.
2nd dec row Patt 13 sts, K2 tog, sl 1, K1, psso, patt 13 sts.
Work 3 rows without shaping. Cont dec in this way twice more. 24 sts. Cont in patt without shaping until 143rd row has been completed, ending with a K row.

Shape back
***Next 2 rows** Patt to last 8 sts,

turn and patt to end.
Next 2 rows Patt to last 16 sts, turn and patt to end.
Next row Patt across all sts
Using A, work 8 rows K1, P1 rib. Cast off loosely in rib.***.

Right back leg
Work as given for right front leg, from ** to **, reversing shaping and working 3rd, 1st, 5th, 2nd and 4th patches. Inc one st at end of next and every alt row 10 times in all, noting that extra sts will be worked in last block of colour. 34 sts. Cont in patt without shaping until 83rd row has been completed, ending with a K row.

Shape crotch
Cast off 2 sts at beg of next row. Work 1 row. Dec one st at beg of next and every alt row 8 times in all. 24 sts. Cont in patt until 149th row has been completed, ending with a K row.

Shape back
Work as given for side from *** to ***, continuing 4th patch.

Left leg
Work 3 sections as given for right leg, reversing all shaping and sequence of patches, as required.

Bib
Using No. 3¼mm (*10*) needles and A, cast on 44 sts.
1st row Using A, (K1, P1) 4 times, patt 28 sts as 1st row of 5th patch, using separate ball of A, (P1, K1) 4 times.
2nd row Using A, (P1, K1) 4 times, patt 28 sts as given for 2nd row of 5th patch, using A, (K1, P1) 4 times.
Cont in this way until 30th row of patch has been completed. Using A, work 8 rows K1, P1 rib across all sts.
Next row Rib 8, cast off 28 sts, rib to end.
Cont in rib on each set of 8 sts until strap is long enough to reach centre back of dungarees, making a buttonhole 2.5cm (*1in*) before casting off as foll:
Next row (buttonhole row) Rib 3 sts, yfwd to make 1, work 2 tog, rib 3 sts.

To make up
Press each part under a damp cloth with a warm iron. Join 3 right leg sections tog including hem and waistband. Join left leg in same way. Press seams. Join front, back and inner leg seams. Turn hems to WS at lower edge and sl st down. St bib in centre of front at top of waist ribbing. Sew elastic inside waistband from each side of bib using casing st. Sew on buttons inside back waist.

Traditional Guernsey fisherman knitting

Fisherman knitting is the name given to seamless jerseys, knitted in a very closely woven fabric similar to a patterned brocade. Because of the fineness of the needles used for this type of knitting, sometimes on as fine a gauge as No. 17, the textured patterns do not stand out in relief as with Aran stitches. The whole purpose is to make a fabric which is virtually windproof and a jersey which will stand up to the constant wear-and-tear of a fisherman's life.

As with many of the folk crafts which have been handed down to us through countless generations, these jerseys were often knitted by the fishermen themselves but were more often lovingly knitted by their womenfolk, in traditional patterns which varied from region to region.

The very name 'jersey', originates from the island of that name. Another name in regular use is a 'guernsey' or 'gansey' as it became known, from the sister island in the same group.

Each port around the coastline of the British Isles has developed its own regional style of fisherman knitting. Some have patterned yokes, others have vertical panels of patterns, some have horizontal bands of patterns, but the original guernseys, which were made purely as hard-wearing working garments, were nearly always made in stocking stitch with very little decoration and always in the traditional colour, navy blue. The more elaborate examples which evolved were kept for Sunday best and in Cornwall they were often referred to as bridal shirts and were knitted by the young women for their betrothed.

A traditional guernsey is knitted entirely without seams, often worked on sets of 5, 6, or even more double-pointed needles. The body is knitted in rounds to the armholes, then instead of dividing the work for the back and front at this point, the work is continued in rounds with the position of the armholes separated from the main sections of

the guernsey by a series of loops wound around the needle on every round. These loops are dropped from the needle on the following round and the process is repeated until the guernsey is the required length. When this section is completed a series of what look like the rungs of a ladder mark each armhole. These loops are cut in the middle and the ends carefully darned into the main fabric, then the sleeve stitches are picked up around the armholes and the sleeve is knitted in rounds down to the cuff. The shoulder stitches are grafted together to finish the garment without one sewn seam.

The shape of these garments is as distinctive as the patterns. They all feature a dropped shoulder line and crew neckline, with little, if any, shaping. Sometimes buttons and buttonholes would be added to one shoulder for ease in dressing and undressing, a gusset made before the armhole division and carried on into the top of the sleeve, or the neck would be continued to form a small collar but the simplicity of the basic design has never been bettered, to give the utmost warmth, freedom of movement and protection to the wearer.

Traditional guernsey
Sizes
To fit 96.5[101.5:106.5:112]cm (38[40:42:44]in) chest

Length to shoulder, 58.5[59.5:61:62]cm (23[23½: 24:24½]in)

Sleeve seam, 45.5cm (18in), adjustable

The figures in brackets [] refer to the 101.5 (40), 106.5 (42) and 112cm (44in) sizes respectively

Tension
28 sts and 36 rows to 10cm (3.9in) over st st worked on No. 3¼mm (10) needles

Materials
14[15:16:17] × 50grm balls of Double Knitting

One set of 4 No. 3¼mm (10) needles pointed at both ends or No. 3¼mm (10) circular Twin Pin

One set of 4 No. 2¾mm (12) needles pointed at both ends or No. 2¾mm (12) circular Twin Pin

Guernsey body
Using set of 4 No. 2¾mm (12) needles cast on 264[276:288:300] sts. Mark beg of round with coloured thread. Cont in rounds of K1, P1 rib for 7.5cm (3in). Change to set of 4 No. 3¼mm (10) needles. Cont in rounds of st st until work measures 33cm (13in) from beg. Commence yoke patt.

1st round P to end.

2nd round K to end.

Rep these 2 rounds twice more, then 1st round once more. **.

***Work 5 rounds st st.

Divide for armholes
1st round *K132[138:144:150] sts, wind yarn 10 times around right hand needle — called loop —, rep from * once more.

Rep last round once more, dropping extra loops from needle before loop 10.

3rd round *K6[9:0:3], (K6, P1, K11, P1, K5) 5[5:6:6] times, K6[9:0:3], drop extra loops, loop 10, rep from * once more.

4th round *K6[9:0:3], (K4, P1, K1, P1, K9, P1, K1, P1, K5) 5[5:6:6] times, K6[9:0:3], drop extra loops, loop 10, rep from * once more.

5th round *K6[9:0:3], (K4, P1, K3, P1, K7, P1, (K1, P1) twice, K3) 5[5:6:6] times, K6[9:0:3], drop extra loops, loop 10, rep from * once more.

6th round *K6[9:0:3], (K2, P1, (K1, P1) 3 times, (K5, P1) twice, K3) 5[5:6:6] times, K6[9:0:3], drop extra loops, loop 10, rep from * once more.

7th round *K6[9:0:3], (K2, P1, K7, P1, K3, P1, (K1, P1) 4 times, K1) 5[5:6:6] times, K6[9:0:3], drop extra loops, loop 10, rep from * once more.

8th round *K6[9:0:3], (P1, (K1, P1) 6 times, K9, P1, K1) 5[5:6:6] times, K6[9:0:3], drop extra loops, loop 10, rep from * once more.

9th round *K6[9:0:3], (P1, K11, P12) 5[5:6:6] times, K6[9:0:3], drop extra loops, loop 10, rep from * once more.

10th round *K6[9:0:3], (P11, K1, P1, K9, P1, K1) 5[5:6:6] times, K6[9:0:3], drop extra loops, loop 10, rep from * once more.

11th round *K6[9:0:3], (K2, P1, K7, P1, K13) 5[5:6:6] times, K6[9:0:3], drop extra loops, loop 10, rep from * once more.

12th round *K6[9:0:3], (K14, P1, K5, P1, K3) 5[5:6:6] times, K6[9:0:3], drop extra loops, loop 10, rep from * once more.

13th round *K6[9:0:3], (K4, P1, K3, P1, K15) 5[5:6:6] times, K6[9:0:3], drop extra loops, loop 10, rep from * once more.

14th round *K6[9:0:3], (K16, P1, K1, P1, K5) 5[5:6:6] times, K6[9:0:3], drop extra loops, loop 10, rep from * once more.

15th and 16th rounds As 1st, dropping extra loops.

Keeping armhole loops correct, work 5 rounds st st, then rep from ** to ** once. ***. Rep from *** to *** once more. Beg with a 2nd row, cont working in patt from ** to ** until work measures 21.5[23:25:25.5]cm (8½[9:9½:10]in) from beg of loops, omitting loop 10 at end of last round. Break off yarn.

Divide for shoulders
Keeping patt correct, sl first and last 35[37:39:41] sts of back and front sections on to holders, knit across each set of 62[64:66:68] sts of neck separately for 6 rows.

Cast off loosely.

Graft shoulder sts from holders.

Sleeves
Cut loops of armholes and darn in ends. Using set of 4 No. 3¼mm (10) needles and with RS of work facing, K up 110[114:118:122] sts round armhole. K 5 round st st, then rep from ** to ** as given for body.

Cont in rounds of st st, dec one st at beg and end of next and every foll 6th round until 74[80:84:88] sts rem. Cont without shaping until sleeve measures 40.5cm (16in) from beg, or required length less 5cm (2in).

Change to set of 4 No. 2¾mm (12) needles. Work 5cm (2in) K1, P1 rib. Cast off in rib.

These designs complete our collection of traditional designs for your pattern library. You will also enjoy the forgotten pleasure of working with natural yarns. We hope you have enjoyed these patterns and that you will now be able to follow even the most complex Aran designs and perhaps design your own.

Index

746.43

AUTHOR

Aran and Fiar Isle knitting

TITLE

746.43
Aran and Fair Isle knitting

DATE DUE		
DEC 5 1988		
APR 0 6 1989		
NOV 0 7 1991		
JAN 0 2 1992		
FEB 2 0 1993		
FEB 1 3 1997		
DEC 2 6 1997		
GAYLORD		PRINTED IN U.S.A.